MENTAL TOUGHNESS

Change Your Mental Models and Boost Your Confidence

(Easy Ways to Build an Unbeatable Mind and Find Success in Life)

Richard Thresher

Published by John Kembrey

Richard Thresher

All Rights Reserved

Mental Toughness: Change Your Mental Models and Boost Your Confidence (Easy Ways to Build an Unbeatable Mind and Find Success in Life)

ISBN 978-1-77485-232-3

All rights reserved. No part of this guide may be reproduced in any form without permission in writing from the publisher except in the case of brief quotations embodied in critical articles or reviews.

Legal & Disclaimer

The information contained in this book is not designed to replace or take the place of any form of medicine or professional medical advice. The information in this book has been provided for educational and entertainment purposes only.

The information contained in this book has been compiled from sources deemed reliable, and it is accurate to the best of the Author's knowledge; however, the Author cannot guarantee its accuracy and validity and cannot be held liable for any errors or omissions. Changes are periodically made to this book. You must consult your doctor or get professional medical advice before using any of the suggested remedies, techniques, or information in this book.

Upon using the information contained in this book, you agree to hold harmless the Author from and against any damages, costs, and expenses, including any legal fees potentially resulting from the application of any of the information provided by this guide. This disclaimer applies to any damages or injury caused by the use and application, whether directly or indirectly, of any advice or information presented, whether for breach of contract, tort, negligence, personal injury, criminal intent, or under any other cause of action.

You agree to accept all risks of using the information presented inside this book. You need to consult a professional medical practitioner in order to ensure you are both able and healthy enough to participate in this program.

TABLE OF CONTENTS

INTRODUCTION 1

CHAPTER 1: THE BENEFITS OF SELF DISCIPLINE 3

CHAPTER 2: THE DEVELOPMENT OF A STRONG MIND 9

CHAPTER 3: THE WARRIOR MENTALITY 23

CHAPTER 4: DEVELOP MENTAL TOUGHNESS 30

CHAPTER 5: MOTIVATION 35

CHAPTER 6: SELF-DISCIPLINE EXPLAINED 41

CHAPTER 7: A PRIMER ON MENTAL TOUGHNESS 49

CHAPTER 8: MORE TECHNIQUES TO ACHIEVE A STRESS FREE LIFE 55

CHAPTER 9: MAINTAINING GOOD BRAIN HEALTH 64

CHAPTER 10: YOUR MINDSET 71

CHAPTER 11: KEEP TRACK OF YOUR PROGRESS 82

CHAPTER 12: SETTING GOALS & MAKING COMMITMENTS 92

CHAPTER 13: SELF-DISCIPLINE IN SCHOOL 102

CHAPTER 14: PRESERVING YOUR MENTAL HEALTH 117

CHAPTER 15: TIME MANAGEMENT **131**

CHAPTER 16: DEVELOPING YOUR DISCIPLINE WITH THESE SIMPLE METHODS **139**

CHAPTER 17: BEING CONTROLLED BY OTHERS **149**

CHAPTER 18: TIPS AND TRICKS **163**

CHAPTER 19: WHERE THERE'S A WILL THERE'S A WAY .. **171**

CHAPTER 20: THE MOST POWERFUL SKILL YOU CAN LEARN: SETTING GOALS **175**

CONCLUSION **182**

Introduction

Your lifestyle defines your character. Your personality and the lifestyle you live are all consequences of your actions. Your habits you've developed over time will determine your fate. They will determine how fast or slow you'll be able to achieve your goals. If you're looking to have a prosperous life, it is essential to establish positive habits that can replace the bad habits you have now. If you do not achieve this, you'll never attain the determination, power, positive attitude and determination you require to achieve your goals and live the life you desire to live.

If you've bought this publication, it's going to assume that you're looking to alter or enhance a part of your life that's difficult to eradicate or implement. I hope that after reading this book, you'll discover ways to begin the process and then adopt the principles you've made a decision to change in your life , to be prosperous in the future.

Chapter 1: The Benefits Of Self Discipline

If you hear "self-discipline," you might imagine thoughts of drill teachers shouting down new recruits at boot camp or maybe Zen monks meditating for days and days. Whatever picture immediately comes to mind, it's the most extreme variant of the idea. Though drill instructors as well as Zen monks represent self-control however, there are other ways to practice self discipline that don't require military instruction or the confinement of the monastery. Self-discipline is something that is achievable and developed by anyone who lives every day life. Self discipline can not only be developed in everyday life however, it could also bring enormous benefits in the everyday world. In the end, a lot of what you do on a every day requires a certain degree of effort from your side. The more disciplined and disciplined you are in your choices, the greater your efforts will be.

One of the reasons the military puts so much emphasis on self-control is that they are aware of the dangers that can occur when someone isn't in control of their actions. The last thing that the military would want to do is issue an extremely dangerous weapon to someone who has lost their keys. That's why instructors go to great measures to 'break' an individual out of their previous routines. Most of the time, fresh recruits in the military are filled with poor and unproductive practices. Only through removing these behaviors can someone be built into an effective, fully accountable member of the military and, consequently, be entrusted with the risky weapons and equipment that they'll be using in their new role. Self-discipline is a broad mental state that is a part of all aspects of one's life after having developed. Therefore, focusing on precisely what you need to do to make your bed or the best way to iron your clothes serves an extremely valuable function. These workouts help develop a self-control that guarantees that one is able to endure even the most challenging of circumstances by staying confident, calm and determined to endure and perhaps even triumph.

Religious institutions have their own motivation for creating self discipline for their pupils. They believe that the lack of self discipline can cause people to fall into the most basic kind of being. Only when people show the courage and determination to fight off temptation or attain higher goals will they be able to achieve the highest level of fulfillment in their lives. This kind of situation is quite extreme and could seem alien to the normal everyday life. However, the underlying reason behind this theory is very relevant to everyday life. If people aren't disciplined in their behavior, they typically look for the easiest route to escape the situation. Although this is an acceptable way to go but it's not the path that leads to any real feeling of satisfaction or achievement. Therefore, just as a monk may seek higher levels of consciousness , or other similar levels by a disciplined and self-controlled lifestyle as well, so can people in general achieve higher levels of achievement by taking an approach that is more disciplined to daily life and the tasks involved.

The most important thing you need to learn about self-discipline, is that it's actually self-serving. At first , it might appear as if all self-discipline is self-sacrifice to benefit other people at your own cost. But the truth is that self-discipline can remove a number of the obstacles you create yourself that prevent you from reaching the degree of achievement and success you desire and merit. So, instead of being self-sacrificing, it is actually self-promotion. When you have gotten rid of all the negative habits and bad attitudes that you are currently displaying, you'll be able to following any goal or any dream you could dream of. Although your new motivation and determination can benefit other people, the reality is that you'll end up being the winner at the end!

There many elements to developing and maintaining a solid sense of self-control, there is none that is as crucial as the one of mental toughness. In the end, if you are not confident of self-worth, or do not have a goal to achieve anything, self-control is probably out of your capabilities. If, however, you have an honest view of yourself or have goals and goals you wish to fulfill You have the qualities required to be self-controlled, and, consequently better able to achieve the goals and goals you have set. Mental toughness is a combination of other factors too, like determination, courage and most importantly, dedication. Once you have these qualities in your head, you'll be capable of building them up by making them stronger and more powerful like a weightlifter who builds their muscles while working out. Even if the elements you are focusing on are weak at first the right practices and habits will allow you to build these elements to new levels at the end. When you've reached mental toughness, your level of self-control will increase.

Chapter 2: The Development Of A Strong Mind

Have you ever looked around at the your society, and thought why people have different positions in terms of their lifestyle?

Have you ever wondered why certain individuals are living an extravagant lifestyle, when the majority of the population lives an ordinary or sub-par lifestyle?

To make it more familiar Have you ever thought about the reason you're in this place right this moment?

The human race has developed into a variety of groups ranging from tribes and race to nationality, race, etc. Social class is one of the categories in the human social interactions, particularly in developing and developed countries. People tend to be more with those who are part of their particular social class.

There are millionaires and billionaires, but the majority of the world's population lives an average or less than the average lifestyle.

The most important factor in everything lies in the brain! It is an part of humans that mostly deals with reasoning and decision-making. It is guided by the soul which is the part that handles emotions.

The development of the mind towards maturity and health is essential for every human being to ensure reaching their goals and goals. Mind is the part which visualizes the achievement of a dream or vision and that is what motivates us to do whatever is required.

But, it's an entirely different matter to know what you need to know and another to do it. The motivation to accomplish what is required that is known as motivation- is referred to as willpower. Willpower is the basis of determination (the willpower to accomplish what it requires) is processed by the mind.

Generally speaking, everything is referred to in the context of Mental Toughness.

Mental toughness also includes the ability to see past obstacles and treat them as stepping stones for the next step of the path to your goal. The process must be completed with a range of obstacles, which mostly are character tests.

People might judge you and criticize your vision and ideas You may be deficient in resources, etc. In this moment, many individuals who haven't developed mental strength are likely to quit and live an ordinary, substandard existence.

Why is it important to build a strong mind? Every human being desires, which is why you are looking at this article because you wish to know what you need to do. The most important thing is to to fulfill your goals. If obstacles are lingering within your head it can be difficult to realize your dreams, however, if you conquer your mind and build determination you will be able to overcome challenges on the outside.

There are many other reasons to build a mental toughness. There are a few of them:

Creativity

If you want to achieve your goals it is essential to be imaginative and unique. A well-rounded mind is capable of thinking outside the box. It is capable of generating innovative ideas and concepts which will benefit humans.

For instance, the inventions in Science-A. Scientists like Thomas Edison figured out that it was important to have a regular method to provide light in dark. His tenacious mind was the reason he began to experiment with the bulb. Although many failed but he did in the end create the first bulb. This invention is believed to be his.

People who have made a lot of progress through their careers in the fields of sciences, music, arts and sports have to be able to do more or find something completely innovative.

Motivation and Determination

As mentioned earlier, motivation is the will to do what you want to do , and determination is the willpower to take the action you need to do. A well-developed mind is able to create these essential elements that will lead to the achievement of goals and dreams.

The power of motivation and determination allows us to challenge our limits and overcome negative influences on our minds.

Persistence and Consistence

A person with a strong mind can work on things over and over until they master it. This is consistency. Persistence is the determination to continue to work hard even when you having to face many difficulties.

A good instance of this is Michael Jordan who was persistence in his practice as his dream was to be an elite basketball player.

He was said to have that he made more than a thousand baskets.

Identity

If you are developing a strong mind, your identity is among the key aspects that need to be dealt with properly. Your identity is more than just the name you have chosen to use. Understanding your identity involves determining the strengths as well as weaknesses of your abilities as well as your strengths and unique character characteristics.

Once this is established you will be able to locate your ideal spot, thus setting your success story. The reason some people get unhappy in their lives is because they've allowed themselves to be defined by others and systems created by the world.

This could be a huge drawback or can put you in a direction that's not your forte and lead to significant frustrations.

There are a myriad of factors which hinder developing a robust mind e.g. emotional abuse, poor diet, consistently under-performing according to your potential and more.

Mental abuse

The brain is at its most active during its earliest stages. The value of a person and their significance is clear when he or she receives constant motivation and encouragement from the people who he/she looks up to.

But, if they experience something else the sense of worth and significance and self-discovery of their talents is severely diminished.

Mental abuse can be characterized as neglect, abuse, and emotional physical and emotional abuse. If someone is intent to build their mental strength and strength, but was subject to violence,

It is recommended to take the initial step of consulting an experienced psychologist or counselor to help them navigate their unconscious recovery.

Nutrition and Exercise

This is among the most crucial areas to be attentive to to help build mental strength. Most people tend to take this issue for granted and have resulted in them losing their accomplishments or hindering their success in the end.

Research has shown that the body consumes approximately 20% of our body's energy, which makes this the organ which uses the most energy when compared to other organs. A healthy diet and exercise can stimulate certain hormones and proteins in the brain that are associated with the brain's performance.

Everything that is related to the fulfillment of your goals and dreams will require a significant involvement of your brain. It is crucial to choose a healthy diet that is suitable for the brain's requirements.

If someone is exhausted following an event that is short-term in brain activity, e.g. writing creative proposals, then they should pay more attention to their diet along with other factors that boost the performance of their brain.

Physical activity can play a significant role in the health of the brain. Its major impact is on the rate at which neurons are created and also the way the neurons are utilized and the length of time they remain.

The frequent involvement of muscles in your body means neuron cells stimulate your brain to be more active through providing neuro-transmission. This improves the neuron pathways and makes them more efficient.

Fitness and nutrition also aid people build a positive self-image and self-confidence in their external surroundings. The reason for this is that an active mind is alert and innovative, which leads to a favorable reputation among your colleagues and peers within a professional setting.

Another benefit is having an attractive, healthy body that isn't weighed down. Your first impression is formed by your appearance. Obesity and weight issues can affect a person's professional image.

Studies have revealed that obese people are more likely to be absent from work due to issues such as obesity associated diseases and ailments (heart and chest issues stress, anxiety, and heart problems) as well as oversleeping.

Exercise and nutrition are essential to the growth of healthy brains as well as mental toughness.

The above mentioned factors are just some of the causes that mental strength of an individual is diminished. People who suffer from this have a difficult time in our current society which is the reason we have all the reasons to live in a world that is not up to par.

It is because they can't mix in with the areas where radicle brain activities are involved in any way, whether professionally or academically. Here are a few negative effects of a weak mind:

Laxity and Laziness

Laxity can be defined as a lack of care: not taking care of the things that surround you. It is inextricably linked with lazyness, which is the inability to things, do something or exert efforts.

This happens when we allow negative forces in our minds to guide our decisions. A strong mind is capable of rising above or simply ignore them completely. It is possible to have a fantastic idea, but have no intent to take action on it.

In times where lazy people do not are thinking about the technicalities involved in achieving success, they simply sit back and relax. This is a risky approach to living as all human beings are equipped to work to earn a living.

The development of a healthy mindset will push your feet and hands to take action. Every action results in another and this forms the basis of the success.

Conformity and Stagnation

The definition of conformity is that you are a part of a specific field that isn't your area of expertise. Research has revealed that a lot of individuals in the workplace are dissatisfied with the way they earn their sources of earning.

This is due to the fact that they go through the system, e.g. the educational system and let it take them to wherever they want without considering what they want to accomplish or what they'd like to go. This is not meant to denigrate or ignore the importance of education.

It is recommended to obtain an education, but even better to go to school in a subject of your choice. It is always beneficial to think outside of the box and not be afraid of failing.

Sometimes, negative people force us to comply with the rules they've imposed on us. Consider an example of an employee who asks their boss for permission to leave their job so they can begin their own company. The boss could respond with negative comments e.g. how difficult it is to succeed in the business world.

They may even take it personal, slamming your convictions. Someone with a weak-willed mind is likely to return to work in a state of discontent and embarrassment. It can lead to Stagnation.

A positive mind will guide an individual to forget about negative feelings and act as they think is most beneficial for the improvement of their own lives.

Inadequate or diminished of the goal

When a person has defined their goals, goals, and goals and goals, they are now able to define their discovered purpose. But, someone with a weak mind might be unable to articulate their goals because they could seem to be impossible to accomplish.

Some may be able to identify the goals, but obstacles might cause them to abandon their goals that they have clearly laid out.

Low Self-esteem

Self-confidence is a significant factor in achieving your goals. In the event that you come up with a fantastic idea, it's time to put it into an idea. How do you explain it to the large people who want to help fund and encourage the idea if you don't trust your own idea?

Self-esteem issues can lead to more problems like low self-esteem and lack of confidence, among others. A strong-willed person can hold their own in high places, as they strive to reach amazing places with regard to their ambitions.

A lack of mental toughness is a cause of some really sad outcomes that can cause frustrations and issues such as depression. It is essential to establish the strength of your will, clear judgement and a sane, purposeful lifestyle.

Chapter 3: The Warrior Mentality

"Being a warrior is not about the act of fighting. It's about being so prepared to face a challenge and believing so strongly in the cause you are fighting for that you refuse to quit."
- Richard Machowicz, Author of "Unleash the Warrior Within"

It is often said that sports are like combat or war that is absurd. However, one possible parallel drawn is the warrior mindset of soldiers and athletes. Warriors are known for their mental strength and knowing how they build that resilience is something that could be utilized to enhance the training of athletes in the fights they'll have to fight.

Navy Seal Training

It's not a secret that the most mentally tough people on earth are those who undergo the intense training offered by The Navy Seals Program. Due to the demanding and extremely dangerous missions that these soldiers are required to complete in the course of their work It is essential that they be both brave and unaffected by the negative effects of fear.

The secret of learning lies within the process of habituation. It is a type of learning where the subject is less likely or not able to react to stimulus following repeated exposure. For the Navy Seals it means that the longer you expose soldiers to things they're initially scared of it is possible to eventually train them to get over the anxiety. Interview with Men's Health Magazine, Sergeant Bill Cullen of the First Battalion of the Fourth Marines put it this in this way "Essentially you're altering the body's program to manage its hardware. It can be done while standing over an 18th green. It is able to make a last-second free throw. It can be used to knock through a door, with an enemy on the opposite side."

In addition, though being physically fit is an essential part of being an Navy Seal however, it's only an essential requirement for those who wish to join this elite group. The most important thing is the mental part. People who are perceived to be mental weak will be the first who are eliminated regardless of how impressive the physical stats are. Lieutenant Colonel Eric Potterat made an interesting connection with Navy Seal candidates and Olympic athletes. "Physically there's a very small difference between those who take home Olympic gold as well as the rest of the field. It's similar to the SEAL candidates that we're seeing here. Amazing equipment. Push-ups, sit-ups, running swimming, out of the ordinary and incredible. However, in the Olympic center, sports psychologists discovered there is a difference in winning a medal and none is determined by the athlete's mental abilities. The top athletes, Tiger Woods Kobe Bryants, Michael Jordans -- that's what sets them apart from the athletes. Understanding how to make use of information."

In essence, what it is about for superior soldiers is, by constantly placing themselves in challenging conditions or stressful situations regularly during training, they develop their minds so that they do not have an emotional connection to risk. They become more numb to anxiety and are more likely to withstand stress.

Spartan Training

"The Spartans say that any army may win while it still has legs under it; the real test comes when all strength is fled and the men must produce victory on will alone."

- Steven Pressfield, Gates of Fire

Personally one of my most cherished films of all time is the one called 300. It tells the tale about The Battle of Thermopylae where a small band of 300 Spartans faced adversity in fighting an attack from the Persian Empire which was said to comprise 1 million soldiers. It is absurd to think that such a feat could be feasible but Spartans weren't just mere soldiers.

In the time of their reign, Spartans were regarded as the most disciplined and powerful warriors of the world. Spartans were recognized for their refusal of things that were perceived to be weak and pursued their training in a single goal: on improving their ability to be effective in battle. One of the most fascinating features of Spartan improvement of mental toughness was taking a bath with cold, icy water.

In Ancient Sparta hot water was regarded as a luxury, and Spartan warriors shunned everything they considered to be luxurious or lazy. Thus, they would indulge in regular baths with frigid water as they believed that it would prepare them to face pain and build a strong spirit. The ability to overpower the mental and physical impact of cold water was a feat of strength and made them stronger mentally to the point where they could tolerate discomfort. If you think about the fact that the typical person would be scared to go through a cold shower It is clear that it requires a robust person to tackle this kind of task.

The key point is that exceptional individuals often perform actions that other people would find insane. However that you can't achieve extraordinary results from ordinary training. Being faced with a situation that you fear because of its nature, helps to build up strength in the body and force the body to adjust. Only through putting oneself to the test and pushing past obstacles is one able to truly grow.

What can we do to apply this knowledge to our young athletes? Of course, we're not planning for the possibility of sending them to battle, but certain concepts are the same. Inviting young athletes to confront their fears with a straight face without allowing themselves just excuse themselves or find an easy route out. The most important thing to take away when looking at how soldiers train to improve their mental strength is that it is able to be built. Mental toughness isn't simply something you're given, it is a quality that can be substantially improved through the proper training.

Chapter 4: Develop Mental Toughness

How do you define mental toughness?
Mental toughness is the ability to take advantage of the psychosomatic edge , which allows the person to work at intensity and effectiveness in the rigors put on them in the course of competition, training, interplay with their inner dialogue. Particularly, when the stresses are severe or the circumstances are threatening. Anytime there are demands that are highest when the characteristics of mental strength are the most evident.

Three key factors in developing mental toughness were revealed by an ex Navy SEAL as well as Navy SEAL trainer, Phil Black. These secrets, which are closely guarded, can help you develop higher levels of mental strength and help you dominate your sport and training. They are simple to learn and are also extremely efficient and utilized to some top athletes in the world.

Many aspects to mental fitness and mental strength however the fundamentals are straightforward and can be broken down into a set of fundamental elements. It doesn't matter if you're used in sports such as tennis, basketball, baseball or boxing. For fitness, it could be weight lifting, running or even martial arts. These concepts for mental health, and the psychological aspects of it, can be utilized in any discipline.

What is mental toughness? Mental toughness is the capacity to persevere through events which go wrong, or which can be strenuous and/or difficult. It's the capacity to keep your inner dialog (your internal dialogue) positive in spite of the negative external circumstances.

When you were born to the age of 18 you were taught "no" 150,000 times. That's 700 times a month or 22 times in a every day! People say, "No, get away from there" and "Stop doing that". Certain of these were meant to protect you from danger, and some were to stop you from growing because of the fears of others or inexperience.

This makes you vulnerable to negative influences. Psychologists have discovered that 77% of internal self-talk is negative , and opposing. Are you aware of the extent to which our abilities are hindered?

I am sure you've been told that there are no limitations on what we can be, be and do. This number shows quite evidently our own limitations who hinder ourselves much more than everything else!

So, you have to control your thoughts or "they" will do it for you. The way Navy SEALs have accomplished it:

Be aware of your self-talk, the internal dialogue you tell yourself each day. Take note of what is going on in your thoughts. Are you surrounded by positive thoughts as well as negative? What do you feel like on a daily and moment-to-moment basis?

Are you contributing to the negative or to the positive side? Two days in a row, note everything that is negative for up to 48 hours. Only your negative thoughts. You need to realize the amount of what you are thinking about is negative. Psychologists have discovered that, on average, 77% of your inner speech is negative. What percentage of yours is it?

Eliminate negative thoughts and thoughts. What type of content do you study? What kind types of individuals do you have a relationship with? Do you often laugh with your friends? This can be a sign how the situation is going. Be aware of what you allow to enter your brain, and apply a filter and block out any negative influences. Your surroundings and the people with whom you interact and the information you listen to or read influence how you think. When you are in a positive, positive environment it's much more able to handle any storm that may come.

Reframe any negative event in a positive way. Utilize the humor in your life, and your brain will interpret it in a different way. Even if something isn't good does not mean you must accept it this way. The majority of your life's challenges are the way you react to it. If your training is tough or demanding, then you might think, "Ha! Ha! This workout is killing me, is this all there is? I want some more, I'm just warming up. I'm tougher than all of this, you can't defeat me!"

Chapter 5: Motivation

Depression sufferers generally aren't motivated to pursue any other goal. Whatever your objectives are, goals can provide motivation. For instance, if dislike being in a group you can set yourself a goal similar to the ones shown below:

Today, I'm going to go out and meet with a friend.

Today I am going to go to a friend's house

Today I'm going to ensure that I engage with 2 other people

The goal should be precise and must be something that you know to be your weak point. If you're overweight, you can establish goals to help you:

Today, I'll eat a healthy meals for lunch.

Today I'm eating an apple

Today, I'm going to weigh myself.

If you don't have any motivation, it's impossible to transform your mindset from a negative one to positive one. However, your goals should be tangible instead of generalizations. For instance, if you were to declare "I will lose weight one day" it's not specific enough and gives you the power to delay the process since it's possible that "one day" may never be able to come.

Every person needs a motivation and if you're not motivated then you should think of goals that seem simple, and gradually increase them more difficult and experience the satisfaction you feel when you accomplish the desired goal.

One of the most effective ways to boost self-esteem is volunteering. It is the act of setting aside a small portion of your time to assist others. What this means is that you will come out of an experience similar to the feeling that you've made a difference and did something nice to others. This is an excellent tool to boost your self-esteem. Even even if you only help serve meals at an area soup kitchen the thing you're learning is to be able to give and not expect anything back. It's crucial because what you get from it will boost confidence in yourself. You're happy with yourself , and that's something you can build upon. Encourage yourself to perform each day a little kindness with no expectation of gratitude and not expecting the entire world to love your actions. The opinions of the world don't really matter. You must live with your own perception of your self and that's what's keeping you from moving forward right now.

Make yourself task-oriented for the near term. For instance What do you plan to accomplish this morning? What are you planning to do this afternoon? Set your goals in terms of things that you are able to achieve, then gradually ramp up the challenge to make sure you remain focused and work towards getting there. On television there are people who fight against the odds , and in the final moments of their day, the only thing they have to motivate themselves is to change their character. If you get up in the morning with no motivation, it's likely that you'll never achieve anything. If you're always thinking about your past mistakes and comparing yourself to these - it's the time to step back and begin to establish new goals.

Today, I'm going to work.

Today, I'll clean the kitchen.

Today, I'm going to tackle my hair

Today, I'm applying for an employment opportunity.

Today, I'll walk the dog of the neighbor's neighbor. walks

Depression sufferers often slip in a state of confusion due to the fact that they lack motivation or commitments, which could hinder your progress. Make a list of your daily goals and reach these goals because these plans will allow you feel that you've achieved something from your day. It's satisfying when you've set yourself an objective and achieved it. And then, you can celebrate the accomplishment. Be gentle with yourself and revel in your successes.

It is essential to find motivation and to be able to see what you accomplish as the achievements add up, and feed your brain with positive energy. If you can repeat positive thoughts as your routine, you'll be amazed at how it can change your life. Habits are the things that people develop throughout their lives. The presence of depression or stressed indicates that your established habits are not positive. Change them into positive habits by motivating yourself to accomplish the tasks you do, and rewarding yourself for your accomplishments. This way, you'll be an individual success to yourself and that's what's important. It doesn't matter how other people view your character. If you're a person with positive attitudes towards your life, you'll discover that people will appreciate you for it, which will cause your lifestyle to transform to the better.

All you need is some motivation and goals will really help since you are able to see the progress you've made and you can determine your own level of success.

Chapter 6: Self-Discipline Explained

Time is among the most precious resources we can avail If we do not use time, we risk losing a chance that could alter our lives. This may sound a bit dramatic, but however, it's the truth. The time can pass by in a flash of an eye, and in a matter of minutes you'll get to a point at which you look back on your life and question what you did to allow it in a blur and not achieving the success you could be able to. It's interesting that even though we all have 60 minutes each hour, all day long and the same amount of days in a calendar month, and throughout the year we are different in our levels of success in various aspects that we live in. Some seem to have everything planned out, while others appear to be completely messed up and some are somewhere have a middle ground. What is the difference between people who appear to have everything in order and those who do not have everything in order? Let me tell you that the combination of self-discipline and habits could be what determines where we can excel in or struggle with in our lives. If you lack the discipline to get things accomplished, and then pair it with bad habits your chances of succeeding in your life are slim. However, with the right attitude and habits with discipline, you will be able to get everything you want in life: a fulfilling relationship, a prosperous work, a lucrative business as well as a fit and healthy body, excellent grades, financial freedom , etc.

But what's your first reaction when you hear "self-discipline"? Do you instantly scream because you believe that self-discipline means that you'll need to give up some of things you cherish and appreciate in exchange for stricter living governed by unending rules?

Believe that self-control isn't as bad as you believe it to be. Sure, sacrifices and adjustments are going to have to be done, but in the end self-discipline is about being more in control of your impulses and desires and also strengthening the part of you that is weak so you are better equipped to conquer your weak points. Self-discipline is the practice of strengthening your inner strength, building it up in the hope that, eventually, you'll become more in control over all aspects of your life, from how you respond to specific situations to how you respond to the challenges that arise in your daily life.

See? It's not so bad as you thought It's not, isn't?

Why Do I Need Self-Discipline in My Life?

It's easy to understand that you require self-control because it'll aid you in becoming more successful in your life. There's a good reason that a lot individuals who have the highest success individuals worldwide have attributed their success to self-discipline since it's an essential skill that every person must possess. It's not intended to take away enjoyment by forcing you to live a less restrictive and controlled lifestyle than you'd prefer. It's intended to assist you in staying in the right direction to reach your goals and reach your maximum potential. Without the extra boost, that crucial kick in the back and tummy, we'd be guilty of taking a break way too much and enjoying the easy way. Who would be willing to put in many hours working or giving up the things they'd like to accomplish, in the event that they were given the option of not doing it? Right?

Everyone could benefit from having a bit of discipline in their lives. If you have children It is recommended to start them off early by making sure you enforce this habit right from the beginning. If you're an older adult who's struggled to get work completed and remain focused there's still time to start turning things around.

Here are some reasons you require discipline in your daily life:

This makes it easier to stay with your choice and follow it through until the end, instead of giving up halfway through.

It gives you the additional determination to stick through whatever you do.

It helps you control your impulses It also makes you less likely to surrender to your urges in the name of immediate satisfaction.

It can help you understand why must make the sacrifices that you're making right now to accomplish the goals you'd like to accomplish.

When you accomplish an objective or landmark through discipline this gives you that feeling in confidence, self-esteem, joy and satisfaction that you've achieved something worthwhile.

It helps you avoid being impulsive.

It can help you establish positive habits of living that will benefit you greatly in the long run.

It can help you get the most out of the time you've been given to reach your maximum potential.

It will help you remain focused. People who have succeeded have achieved this by staying committed to their goals, and their self-control will never allow them to wander off from the path they've chosen until they've attained what they desire. It requires intense, unwavering concentration to stay on the right the right track.

You accomplish things.

It makes you realize that you're capable of doing whatever you put the intention of.

It helps you to overcome the habit of procrastination.

Instant gratification is among the biggest enemies of life and is the main reason why we are unable to stay on the path towards achieving success. The idea of having the ability to enjoy pleasure right now instead of waiting for the pleasure to appear in the near future is one which not all can overcome. It wouldn't happen if weren't armed with discipline to guide us on the path.

Do you understand why we must be disciplined to live our lives? There's a lot to gain and nothing to lose when you adopt this highly effective routine. Sure, it'll be challenging at first - as any new lifestyle and adjustment adjustments aren't easy - but believe me, when it's completed and done you'll be extremely happy for having done this.

As I've already mentioned the secret to success lies in having the correct habits that will propel you to success , and unbeatable discipline. The following quote from Will Durant sums it all:

"We are what we repeatedly do. Excellence, then, is not an act, but a habit."

Then I'll go further and put it in this manner:

"We have what it takes to do the things we consistently do. It isn't a single act, but rather a combination of good habits, and unbeatable levels of self-control."

Discipline and discipline can help you become more efficient in your life, i.e. accomplish more within a shorter amount of time. This eventually increases your chances of success in your life. If you are able to combine it with mental toughness that allows you to adhere to your plan or goals You can be certain that your efficiency will be extremely high. However, before you can learn to become productive, relying the power of self-control and mental toughness, it's essential to comprehend what you're doing. Let's look at that in the next.

Chapter 7: A Primer On Mental Toughness

What is the first thing that comes to your mind when you hear "mentally tough"? In most cases you imagine those who don't collapse easily, but is actually victorious when faced with adversity. If you're a lover of any kind and you think of the mental strength of athletes who've performed superbly even when they're in a tough position, for instance, they've lost a few games or are suffering from the consequences of injuries. Whatever way you interpret the concept, it's crucial to gain a greater understanding of what it means before getting into the details in this book.

What Is Mental Toughness?

Mental toughness isn't just a singular characteristic, but rather a collection of characteristics that allow people to face challenging situations without placing an undue strain on their confidence in themselves. This broad concept has resulted in the word being used to refer to any set of positive characteristics which can assist someone in dealing difficult circumstances. In simple terms If you're mentally tough, you don't stop - you'll always be able to finish your plan of action, even when you face obstacles that need to be dealt with.

What Influences Our Mental Drive and Capacity

There's plenty of research on mental toughness, however up to now, there is no agreement on the nature of it and how it is created. There are some who believe that genetics plays a part in this, however research has not yet established this as the case. The one thing that experts have in common is the notion that the environment an individual lives in plays significant influence on becoming more focused. A well-known research studies on this is Richard Dienstbier's "Theory of

Physiological Toughness" in which he explains that mental toughness can be influenced by four aspects such as early childhood experiences active and passive physical toughening, progressive aging, and passive.

To briefly explain the concept, Dienstbier advocated for the positive physiological effects of stressful circumstances, stating that the subjects (humans as well as animals) changing into "tougher". That "toughness" (or mental toughness in the context of the book) is because the stress response supposedly gives their immune system an extra boost. This also increased their capacity to adjust and, later on manage stress-inducing situations.

Here is a brief explanation of all four elements that influence mental toughness

Childhood experiences - Research conducted on various species of animals observed that stress exposure at an early age resulted in subjects being more resilient. They showed decreased fear when faced with stressors in addition, the adrenal glands (organ that regulates reactions to adverse circumstances) were developed. These all indicated that they were becoming "tougher" over time. Dienstbier concluded that the results of these studies could be applied to human beings. The conclusion, however, isn't a big surprise to many as our personality traits are heavily influenced by the events that is happening in our the early years of our lives.

The process of active toughening or mental strength is a skill that can be developed by continuous exposure to stressful situations. Many consider this idea to be "hardening." It is important to remember that the term "stressors" does not only mean situations that trigger negative emotions. It could also refer to situations that stress the body, or to test your limits. An additional study revealed that those who exercise regularly enhance their physical and thus their mental strength. The coaches of sports are aware of this and they make use of this information to aid their athletes in becoming stronger mentally by implementing properly-designed training and exercise routines.

Passive toughening - Infrequent and unintentional exposure to stressful circumstances can result in increased physical and mental endurance. It hinders the reduction of stress hormones like adrenaline, which keeps you alert and ensures you can get a more effective response to difficult situations. In a way is similar to the second factor that is exposure to stressors in the beginning of life, in the sense that there is a degree of involuntaryness. However, the difference is that time and this is an aspect of the exposure that occurs through one's life.

Progressive Aging - In contrast to the other three aspects, aging makes you more prone to stress, which in turn reduces your mental acuity. Studies have shown that aging causes noradrenaline (neurotransmitter hormone that is involved in the ability to respond and fear) and levels of adrenaline to diminish which results in a less responsive response to stress.

Chapter 8: More Techniques To Achieve A Stress Free Life

There are more ways to try
Body scans and meditations to aid relief from stress
The body scan is comparable to deep body relaxation technique. The but instead of tensing your muscles and relaxing them it is important to concentrate on the sensations in your body.
Practice body scan meditation:
Relax on your back, and ensure that your legs are not crossed. Keep your eyes closed or open and your arms relaxed by your side. Keep your attention on your breathing and allow your belly to move up and down while you breathe in and out. Continue to breathe slowly for two minutes until you begin feeling relaxed and relaxed.
Then, as you shift your attention on the toes of your right foot. Try to note any

sensations that you feel. While doing this, continue to pay attention to your breathing. Keep your eyes on your toes and imagine every deep breath flowing over your toes.

Concentrate on the sole of your left foot. as in the previous exercise Keep your attention on only the heel of the right shoe, and at the same time , the focus on your breath. After a couple of minutes, shift your focus towards your ankle, and then to your calf, knee the thigh, hip, and calf. Moving your body up and repeat this for each body part.

After you have completed the entire body scan, you can relax for a few minutes in quiet and quiet. Take a moment to open your eyes and observe the way your body is feeling.

Mindfulness to ease stress

Mindfulness is the process that allows you to observe your current experience as both internal and external. Stressing over your past or the future usually leads to stress. However, mindfulness helps you focus on the present moment and helps keep you feel calm.

Meditation practice with mindfulness

A calm environment: Pick a peaceful space like the office, garden, home or an outdoor area in which you feel at ease.

Sit comfortably: Relax in an armchair or even on the ground. It is also possible to try the lotsus posture or crossed-legged

Focus: Select a point of focus. It could be a fictional scene, a emotion or a meaningful word or phrase you repeat during your meditation. Maintain your focus if would like to concentrate on an object nearby.

Attitude: If in your mindfulness meditation, another thought comes into your mind, don't be frustrated and instead, gently shift your focus to meditation.

You can practice mindfulness while walking, exercising or eating. Regularly practicing mindfulness can help reduce overwhelming stress.

Visualization technique to relieve stress

Visualization is distinct from traditional meditation. It involves the senses of touch, visual scent, taste, and the sound. Visualization involves imagining or visualizing the scene that will make you feel calm and relaxed at ease, free from any tension or anxiety. You can do visualization-meditation on your own in silence or while listening to an audio recording of a therapist. You may also choose an audio that matches your vision, like the that of waves like.

Practicing visualization

Find a quiet, relax place. Some beginners to the technique of visualization get tired, so sit or stand. Take a deep breath and imagine that all your worries are fading away. Imagine that you are in a tranquil location. Imagine as vividly as can, everything you be able to feel, perceive, hear, and smell. Visualization is most effective when you use all five senses. Do not use images that are suggested by others Use images that naturally relaxes you.

If you're thinking about lakes in the mountains

Take a slow stroll towards the lake , taking note of the textures and colors all around you.

Get involved in all of your senses, one at a time.

Check out the sky and observe the clouds.

You can hear the birds singing close to you.

Take a sniff of the trees

Feel the cool water touch your feet

Savour the clean, fresh air

Feel the sensation of complete relaxation by using the technique of visualization. Once you are at ease, you can open your eyes and return to your reality. Do not worry if you've lost focus in your visualization. If you feel heavyness in your legs or hands, it's normal, and you shouldn't be worried.

Tai chi and yoga to relieve stress

Yoga is a sequence of stationary and moving posesthat are combined with deep breathing. Yoga increases flexibility, strength as well as balance, stamina, and decreases anxiety and stress. Through regular practice, yoga improves muscles that relax. For beginners, starting yoga can be challenging and the chances of injury are higher. Therefore, join an online yoga class, or hire an individual instructor or follow the video instruction.

The best yoga to relieve stress

Yoga poses that incorporate slow breathing, gentle stretching, and steady movement are the best to help relieve stress.

Satyananda: Satyananda is a traditional yoga practice that includes deep relaxation, meditation and gentle postures. Anyone who is looking to begin yoga can benefit from this yoga class for you.

Hatha yoga: Hatha yoga also suitable for beginners.

Power yoga is ideal to those seeking relaxation and stimulation.

Tai chi

Tai chi is a form of flowing, self-paced non-competitive, slow body movements. The movements focus on calmness, concentration, and the conscious flow of vital energy throughout the body. Tai chi used to be an element of martial arts. However, nowadays, tai chi is utilized as a relaxation method to relax the mind while reducing stress and strengthening the body. Like mindfulness meditation, tai-chi helps concentrates on breathing with calmness and focusing on this moment. Tai chi is an easy and safe alternative for all ages. Even those who are recovering from injuries may practice Tai Chi, similar to yoga. You must master the basics by engaging in Tai chi with other people.

Include relaxation techniques as part of your everyday routine

The best method to learn relaxation techniques is to incorporate it into your routine, and then practice it regularly.

Tips for bringing relaxation into your daily routine

Do it in the first hour of the morning: Establish an established time for relaxing techniques, but preferably early in the early morning. Do your relaxation prior to when other obligations and projects get out of your way.

While you're distracted by other tasks Take a moment to meditate during your commutes in the morning or evening, or while you wait in lines and waiting to get a dental appointment. When you're trimming the lawn or working on your house Try deep breathing. Try mindfulness when taking a walk to the car, working out with your dog, or climbing the steps at work. Tai chi can be practiced at the park or in your workplace at lunchtime.

Mix exercise and mindfulness while exercising, you can do some mindfulness exercises instead of watching television.

Do not practice relaxation when you're tired: Try relaxation techniques only when you are awake and alert, exercising while asleep will not be very helpful to you. Do not practice while taking alcohol, tobacco, or drugs or after eating a large meal.

Expect setbacks: Be prepared for setbacks, but do not be discouraged by these setbacks. You can practice and succeed.

Exercises that are rhythmic, like rowing, walking, or running, are the most efficient when you do them with a relaxed mind.

Chapter 9: Maintaining Good Brain Health

There are some simple exercises you can take part in to ensure your brain's health. This can be divided into two aspects that control the physical factors that age us and using methods to improve your mental fitness. In this chapter, we will go into both in sufficient detail to allow you to keep your mental health to its peak.

Taking care over time

To avoid extreme changes in the structure of the brain as we age Here are some preventive actions you can take advantage of:

* Manage risk factors: There are many chronic diseases like heart disease and diabetes that can create lots of stress to the brain. Controlling these conditions will lower the chance of developing cognitive decline in a significant way. If you can maintain your blood pressure as well as your cholesterol levels, you'll be able stop

any decline in brain's function because of physical ailments.

Maintain your exercise levels high. Regular exercise can aid in maintaining mental well-being. Like we said, physical activity triggers an increase in endorphins which help to manage anxiety and other mental disorders. If you can keep your fitness levels up as well, the amount of oxygen available to your brain grows. This stops the degeneration caused by free radicals too. The body detoxifies itself by physical exercises, allowing you to function more effectively mentally.

Eat well: your diet should consist of a variety of foods, including vegetables and fruits. They have all the nutrients crucial to maintain your brain functioning at its best. They also aid in regulating various bodily functions like hormone production and assist the brain deal with the changes in the brain that come as we age. In the event of a injuries, it's healthy to eat a balanced diet and have the supply of nutrients that allow your brain to be more flexible. It is also easier to heal when your brain is stocked with every nutrient it needs. This will help keep inflammations at bay in the future.

Keep in touch with your loved ones and family members People you are passionate about can have a positive impact on your mental wellbeing. If you're constantly around people that you like your brain can to deal with stress better. Additionally, you are able to produce a lot of endorphins when you're within a comfortable and relaxed space. Socializing also requires you to be alert and mentally active to be able to effectively communicate and maintain relationships. This allows you to keep your mental health as you get older. Try to be in a good group and remain content throughout your life.

Apart from these preventive measures there are a variety of other techniques that have been proven to help maintain a healthy mental state. In the next section of this article we will discuss these methods. These are all basic methods that need to be implemented with perseverance.

Techniques for good mental health

Here are some tested methods to maintain your mental health at its peak. These techniques help improve your cognitive skills, helping you to retain more information and then concentrate on routing that information to make your brain more alert and active.

* Habits and mental discipline Mental discipline is a intricate aspects such as self-control. You can enhance the mental discipline of your children by directing your actions toward it. For example you should make it a priority to practice any relaxing method like yoga or meditation that helps you focus on areas such as willpower and self-control. It is also possible to develop good habits such as playing games or taking a daily reading break. These practices will help keep your

mind active and engaged which will improve your mental health.

* Memory strengthening exercises: Be engaged in games and puzzles which improve your memory. There are many games that rely on trivia, and even visualization to assist you in improving your memory. Books that include these games and puzzles are easily accessible. You can also search for many of these games through the web. Regularly playing these games on a daily on a regular basis can help develop your memory.

Increase mental stamina: The most effective way to increase your mental stamina and the brain's capacity to handle stress is to control your thoughts. Engage in positive thoughts , and utilize the method of affirmation that is positive. Pay attention to how you interact with yourself. Be sure that your self-talk builds confidence and makes you feel satisfied and happy. This can help strengthen neurons. It is as easy as creating a list of positive things about yourself, and then reading the list over and over.

Make an habit of learning something new each day: Experiences with new people are essential to a healthy mental well-being. Try to learn or try something new each day. According to the research carried out by the Franklin Institute, new activities aid in improving your memory. They also help your brain to be able to learn new concepts and access this information quicker. If you relocate to a new location or try a different type of food, or learn something new your brain needs to perform a variety of complicated tasks in order to comprehend and process this new knowledge. It's almost an exercise that will strengthen your brain!

* Concentrate on one thing at a given time: People consider multitasking to be an excellent method to increase mental stamina. Sure, it is possible to get a variety of tasks accomplished at the same time. However, the brain does not have the

ability to focus in a specific direction, or a capability that can be honed when you are multitasking. It is best to concentrate on a single item at a time. This will not only improve your cognitive abilities but can also make you more productive because it lets you focus on the larger perspective.

* Exercises for mental dexterity Studies have proven that mental dexterity exercises could transform the way you see the world. They can help improve the neural pathways. Additionally the activities are an effective way to break routines and keeping your brain active and healthy for longer.

Once you start to reap the benefits of a healthy physical fitness It will soon become an integral aspect of your everyday life. The tasks your brain needs are easy to do. All you have to do is incorporate them into your routine, and you'll be capable of making maximum use of your brain's capabilities.

Chapter 10: Your Mindset

It's a bit frustrating to realize to realize that among the crucial abilities you have and which will propel you to the peak of your accomplishment is the one thing that is so hard to keep as a routine.

There may have been times when you've shown self-control in order to obtain something you'd like However, maintaining that focus throughout every day is where battle starts.

Why is it so difficult? It's simple that it takes exertion. It's not easy to anyone. Discipline is something that you must work at which is the reason it's so difficult to keep and maintain.

People who are successful and productive do not simply happen to be born this way. They have that status because they are willing to take risks and sacrifices which others would not. They had to put in the effort to maintain their self-control and are striving to improve it each day. If you'd like to become as them, you're going to have to do the work. There aren't any shortcuts to success.

One thing that can help you get there however, is the awareness of your goals as well as the desire to do the effort that will lead you closer to your goals. It's so easy to declare that you're looking for something, but when achieving what you want takes too laborious then you give up and say, "this is not worth the effort."

It's about Mind over Matter

The next step in the process is likely to be the most, if not the most important aspects of the whole self-discipline procedure controlling your thoughts.

Your mind is an extremely powerful weapon. Actually, your mind is the most powerful weapon you have. It is able to propel you up to new heights, or reverse the process. Many people have difficulty to turn even the most basic of goals come to fruition, while others are pushing the boundaries and redefining their lives since negativity is something that you constantly fight. The issue with negativity is the amount of an impact it can have and the amount of influence it has If you let yourself be influenced by it for long enough it can result in defeat, even before you've taken the first step to start.

Certain people's accomplishments cause you to think "Wow! How did they achieve that? I'm not sure!" The truth is you might be able to in the same way, and by learning how to manage your thoughts and believing that all situations come down to the mind and not matter it is possible to be successful in achieving the same or more results.

What exactly is an optimistic mindset contribute to your efforts to become more disciplined? It is important since developing a positive resilient mindset

Improves your self-confidence

Increases your resilience as having a strong mindset is a sign that you are determined and grit until there is nothing that can stop you from pursuing your goals

Allows you to take every step with confidence This is something that can only happen over time , but is triggered by developing a tough mindset.

You are motivated to continue

Improves your concentration

Reduces stress This can reduce stress. Knowing that you're strong enough to withstand any storm can be a powerful motivator. If you're strong you don't let things take over your life because you realize that deep down that you're in this, and that the adversity you face is just temporary. Being less stressed out about your life will also help improve the overall quality of your life, which leads to more restful sleep, peace of head as well as happiness which starts the moment you make the decision to believe in yourself and remain tough.

Making your mind shift to Positive One

A variety of factors influence how a person succeeds in reaching their goals (self-discipline is one of them). Controlling your thoughts is another aspect. When your thoughts are capable of complaining or becoming negative without being aware of it, then you should definitely begin to control your thoughts so that it moves to the opposite side of the spectrum.

A positive outlook is essential to be successful in all aspects of life. It is the energy that keeps you up and going. Positive thinking also provides a daily dose of inspiration when you are working to build more positive mental attitudes.

How to Build a Positive Mindset

The best method to begin creating a positive attitude and begin to control your thoughts early in the day is to get early to something you think motivates you throughout the day.

Have you got a favourite quotation or phrase that inspires you to go an extra mile? Print it and place the print next to your mattress. Make sure that it is one of the first things you look at when you wake up in the early morning.

Don't end there, however. Find positive affirmations on various locations in your home that you're not likely to miss such as on your laptop or on mirrors on the door to your closet, and even on your smartphone! A positive start to your day can help set the mood for the way your day begins and continues.

Second, be aware of the way you speak to yourself. Your self-talk affects your thoughts and feelings, emotions, attitudes and behaviour. Self-talk is simply the various suggestions you make to yourself while contemplating or planning something. For example, thoughts such as "I could do this," or 'I can't accomplish that' is hard', 'What if it fails?' Should I do it or give up?' "Oh, this is fantastic and I'm going to keep doing it' are instances of self-talk. If the majority of it is negative thoughts, it is a reason the reason you are prone to negative thoughts and get easily drawn by your desires.

Naturally, if it is your habit to say to yourself that your goals aren't easy while claiming that doing nothing or watching movies on Netflix is enjoyable and relaxing, you'll be enticed by both. Self-talk that is negative will hinder you and take your attention away from essential things to do. If you continue to feed these thoughts into your mind and then believe them, you will develop unhealthy thoughts which then hinder you from exercising the self-control required to succeed in the world.

Be aware of the negative self-talk you make and each when you notice yourself saying an untruthful comment to yourself or speaking rudely to yourself, be aware of the behaviour. Take a moment and take a deep breath and then come up with an alternative that is more realistically positive for the negative thoughts. If you were thinking, 'I will never lose weight as I continue to give in to my desires', switch the thought to "Well, let's do it again and this time become aware of my inclinations and participate in healthy ways to fight these. Repetition that thought repeatedly with strength and confidence , and you will be able to imprint it into your mind in a way that it becomes an integral part of your belief system.

Make sure that the suggestion is positive however, it should be as realistic as you can so that you're able to believe the suggestion. Instead of saying, "I could lose 10 pounds in five days', you should say that you can successfully lose weight when I make continuous efforts. Be aware of what you say to yourself, and consistently alter the negative ideas to positive ones to remain in control of your thoughts and urges under control and focus on what is required.

Thirdly, examine your negative thoughts to determine their truthfulness. Most of the time, toxic and unconstructive thoughts aren't real and are simply fabricated by your inner critic, the internal voice that is negative and strong that is nourished through the negative self-talk that you engage in. If you think that you're incapable of doing something, ask evidence that proves that you've never done something. If you are worried that you'll be unable to complete a task look up any event that proves this. If you're unable to locate any evidence or facts to support your belief, you discover that the belief is false and you decide to stop believing the idea.

Ask yourself questions that are positive about what you can do to overcome the obstacles. If you are struggling to eat healthy, and that's something you'd like to improve your self-control , think about the habits you must improve upon. If you're bored to adhere to a particular routine, think about ways to make it enjoyable and interesting for you , so that you can discipline yourself, while having fun as well. Your brain is built to give you answers to your questions exactly the manner you ask them. So if you ask yourself , "Will you fail?' you're likely to get many answers to what you can expect to fail at however, if you inquire about how you can be successful you will be given exactly the methods you require to progress and develop.

Your thoughts can also be affected by the people you spend most of your time with.

According to Jim Rohn, self-help author and motivational speaker, once said:

If you spend time with people that have negative influences over you e.g. people who are unable to control themselves or who don't accomplish anything, those who just complain about the unfairness of life and who have difficulty achieving their goals You are more likely to absorb their negative energy and negative thoughts. Be careful to distance yourself from these individuals by not seeing them frequently, not answering calls at work and talking with them about how you're not going to allow their negativity within your life.

While you're at it, find people who can positively influence you. Family members, friends as well as colleagues who boosts your confidence, is a hard worker and motivates you to keep to your goals must be part of your social circle. If you are surrounded by positive, disciplined individuals their enthusiasm and charisma is passed on to you and will assist you in working to achieve your goals.

It is essential to remain well-organized in this area to develop the self-control you require to conquer the obstacles. Every when you notice negative thoughts, you can practice these methods and then kick them out.

Chapter 11: Keep Track Of Your Progress

Making a plan and then attempting to implement it won't get you halfway. If you're not aware that your plan isn't working, you'll be left thinking about how your efforts haven't resulted in outcomes. If this pattern persists, you'll become angry and your confidence levels are also likely to drop. One way to be sure you're on the right path is to monitor your improvement. When you examine your progress, it will be easy to know where you are. This can help you recognize the importance of the time left. Let's say for instance, it's the case that you've completed only a tiny portion of your work at midday, and you have lots of tasks to finish prior to the end of the day. This realization can allow you to plan your coming days in more efficient way. You'll be able to prioritize tasks and make sure that you complete the most crucial jobs completed first. This will help ensure that you're not putting off any vital project to be completed later, which can result in a significant impact. Like I mentioned earlier it is possible to use your breaks to evaluate your accomplishments.

Do not think of this as a lengthy task. The process of reviewing your progress may involve things as simple as taking items off your list once they've been completed. You can add additional details like how well you did the job as well as the time required to complete the task or any issues you faced, etc. These details will assist you in planning your next day more effectively. If you do not be sure the efforts you put into it are directed in the most efficient method, you'll never get the most benefit. This is why it's vital to review regularly your improvement. Let me let you decide on the frequency of reviews. If you're not sure regarding your time management or your delivery, I'd recommend more frequent reviews. This will provide you with an honest assessment and will assist you in adjusting your pace. If you're sure of your focus, then you might do a quick check at the conclusion of your day.

Realize Failures Happen

Everyone hates having to deal with an unexpected setback. However, things will not always happen as planned. To develop more self-control, you are going to be required to be able to speak up when you fall.

Failure can be as easy as not meeting an objective in the course of the day. You could get distracted, then getting back on track, or not meeting the goals you set for yourself in a year or five years.

It's a great feeling to get there, but control isn't something you are able to always have. However, life can get in the way. Your spouse, mother dad, sibling, or spouse might fall ill or require assistance, and your life gets placed on hold. Making it easier to manage the issues that impede your life is where self-control comes into. If you set aside five minutes to focus on your goal, then you've got self-control.

Discomfort Training

It's simple to outline the four initial methods to improve self-discipline but you have to adhere to the plan. You must give up the immediate reward to achieve your goal. There are certain benefits along the way, however, a lot of them could derail you. Once you have establish your goals, you must identify your weaknesses, change your mental attitude, and develop strategies to alter your behavior, you will must undergo the discomfort and training.

We are not a fan of tough things, the ones which make us uncomfortable. We are accustomed to sticking to the familiar, comfortable concepts. We stay away from anything that causes us to feel anxious or worried.

The best method to practice is to be willing to experience a bit of discomfort. Similar to the dish, beginning with a simple task that comes with no rewards is a great way to help yourself achieve the goal, regardless of how you feel.

The fact is that the final purpose has to be to you a lot to follow through with all of it.

Writers often don't like editing yet they need to finish the job in order in order to publish their book.

A builder who is passionate about build must be able to communicate with customers to make money.

Things happen that cause us to feel uncomfortable.

Perhaps, you are hoping to make improvements in your life and you require discipline to achieve your objectives. You might not want to repeat some of the things you've already knew. For instance, if you want to refresh your memory about the languages you've learned and that involves going through hundreds of terms and phrases that you've heard before. It's boring. It can be re-enforced quickly however it's an essential step to advance in the world of language.

Discomfort training involves facing what you are not comfortable with and dealing with it regardless.

An assignment at work can cause anxiety and fear about whether you're qualified or will make someone miserable.

The person who overcomes these feelings and completes the work, and then receives the reward they didn't think they would receive is the one who is happy.

Therefore, accept the discomfort and work to keep moving forward.

Create an incentive system

Who wouldn't like an incentive to begin on their calendar? A well-designed reward system can definitely assist us in starting. The use of a reward system can aid you in these ways:

However much you'd like to put it put off for some time, the reward that is just right around the corner is sure to encourage you to keep to your plan and complete the task.

A reward could be an affirmation. This can therefore aid in establishing healthy behavior.

You don't require an additional person to help motivate you, if you have a the right rewards system.

It is crucial to not be excessively generous with our rewards. To ensure that rewards are fair and fair, it is essential to follow a few basic guidelines, for example:

Make sure that your reward is given out promptly. If you fail to give your reward in a timely manner it is likely that the reason you have an incentive will not be achieved. The reward should be instantaneous when necessary to ensure that you complete your work completed according to timeframe.

Deciding on the amount of reward can play a significant aspect in determining the level of motivation. If you choose to reward yourself with lavish things, you might get distracted from the larger image and then drift from your plan. The extravagant reward could influence your self-control to a greater degree. However it is important to be prudent when applied when choosing your rewards. If you pick a cheap reward, you'll not care about the work you're working on because there's no substantial incentive to inspire you to continue.

Be sure to keep your rewards positive as is possible. If you can count on positive reinforcements to reward you You can utilize it to establish healthy behaviors.

When looking for an incentive, be sure that you do not choose one that's unreasonable. Your reward must be practical and achievable. This is the only way to gain faith in the reward system. Trust in your reward system is essential to ensure that it has any effect on your life. Therefore, you shouldn't let your thoughts be a wild ride as you try to select an incentive.

Don't choose your addictions as the reward. What you're trying to accomplish by removing procrastination from your life will result in greater productivity and discipline. When a change in self-discipline is in your plans the first thing you must be doing is to address your addictions. It is easy to forget about time due to the consuming nature of our addictions. So, it's important that your rewards don't coincide with your addictions.

Your reward should have some significance and a purpose. This is essential to draw your interest. If you are given rewards that aren't worth it and meaningful, you won't be motivated to even begin working toward it.

Create specific rewards. A specific reward could really motivate you, greater than you think. If the reward is specific, you'll be in a position to see it clearly. This can help keep us from the couch and help us concentrate on the task that is at hand. In contrast If it's something that is not a specific reward, you might not be as enthusiastic, as you ought to be about it.

It may sound like work. If you take the time to complete the work you will get is a fully functional reward system that is capable of encouraging you in all kinds of circumstance.

Chapter 12: Setting Goals & Making Commitments

Pros or amateurs no matter what level, there's one thing that all those involved in sports has in common - they realize the importance of setting objectives. Setting goals are crucial for success. Specific goals are better than entering each performance or game with an undefined "I'll do my best" goal.

Goals can be extremely effective as a method of mental warming-up because they engage you in a cognitive way by forcing you to focus on your task while encouraging you to keep going. These factors are a combination that can inspire behavioral change that allows you to go further and be more focused on achieving the goal you made for yourself.

The Secret to Setting the "Right" Kind of Goals

One common misconception regarding planning goals, is that one have to set high standards that you have to meet. While it's fine to set high goals, if you fail to set realistic expectations is when issues begin to develop. Expectations that are too high can result in the opposite effect and make you be less assured. It's not easy to keep in check since you're trying to be the best you can be, yet at the moment, you're wondering whether you're setting your sights too high for such a small period of time.

It's natural to achieve your goals since you're trying to improve your performance as quickly as you are able. More efficient performances increase the chances of winning and that is what you'd like to achieve after having spent an extensive amount of time training and making sacrifices in the sake of improving your performance. It's normal to be ambitious and an aspect that a lot of professional athletes practice, yet the key to setting goals that can be achieved is to not set goals that are excessively high. If your expectations are overly optimistic and unrealistic, you shift your attention to being more focused on results instead of being focused on how you're doing. You get too focused and distracted by your "destination," instead of paying attention to what you can do on the "journey" like you should be.

A method to illustrate this could be to imagine yourself as a participant in an event. The goal you have set is to reduce the time you finish by five minutes in the following race. In order to reach that objective, you have to find out what aspects of your routine you are currently following need altering. It could be that you need to relax or build up the muscles in your legs, alter your body's posture when you run, or even pushing yourself to run more quickly and increase speed as you run. It could be two ideas that pop up in your head as you are thinking about ways to run a bit quicker. The only thing your thoughts right now is cutting down the five minutes to complete your run faster. This is exactly what the issue is of being so focused on the time to finish that you fail to concentrate on your game plan. The lack of thinking process will be able to determine the things that will increase your physical and performance capabilities over time, as you're focused on trying to complete your 5-minute goal earlier and especially in the event that your body may not be prepared to change its routine so quickly.

The key to setting the correct kind of goals, it transpires is not to set your sights excessively high to the point that where you lose your focus on what is most important. Beware of setting yourself up for a crash if your goals don't correspond in relation to the current situation. If your body isn't sufficiently conditioned to speed up your run during an event that will allow you to finish 5 minutes faster, you should don't make that an immediate goal as you'll end up dissatisfied when you don't complete it. Make goals as milestones you want to strive at instead of putting them as "do-or-die" requirements that must be fulfilled immediately.

The Right Approach to Take With Goals

It's true that you don't need to constantly meet your goals, especially in sports. And even more so when they will divert your attention on what you should be focusing on. As you prepare your thoughts for the next game the first question you should be asking yourself is what you have to concentrate on now to allow you to stay present in the moment? What strategies will you require to accomplish the task in front of you? Do I focus on the right things?

These are the questions you ought to be asking before the game to help you prepare mentally for the exercise since it helps you remember and reminds you the things you need to be paying attention to and that's a higher performance, not an all-or-nothing outcome. Don't get ahead of yourself and put aside any expectations as you get ready for the next event as the moment you head to the field with an mindset that I have to achieve the following XXXX or only achieve the XXXX thing, you're not in the proper mindset for optimal performance. The goal doesn't have to be one that is immediate or a result which must be realized in the present or now. This is not the right method to follow since it will frustrate you in the event that you aren't achieving your goals. of achieving what you want.

The most effective way to achieve your goals is to not be ambitious, but to aim higher. Instead of setting a broad objective, set the goal to be a step higher than where you are currently. Once you have achieved the goal, try to improve your performance by a few steps than where you are. You should make it a gradual step toward your goal. Goals are intended to inspire you to to be better by pushing yourself beyond your level of comfort to show that you can improve. The goal should be achievable in order to provide you with something to set your sights on, so that you don't become complacent or satisfied with your current position. It's easy to lose focus and forget the task at hand if you're struggling to exceed your own expectations with each game.

A way to determine if your goal that you've established for yourself correct type of objective is to look to your previous performances and assess the results. Review these accomplishments prior to attempting to establish the next goal. Consider what you've accomplished in the past, and consider how long it took you to reach this. After you've identified your goals consider setting a goal just one step higher than the current level, making it possible and realistically achievable. This goal should encourage you to try a more than you're currently doing however, not so much to overtax your body. Should you be working with a trainer you've worked with frequently seeking their opinion regarding the topic could be a sensible step to follow. Your coach is capable of providing some information from what they have learned about you and your abilities as well as being the ideal person to hold an open discussion with regarding what your next goals should be.

When you set your goals, it's essential to not make comparisons with other athletes. Their situation is not likely to be similar to yours, and their path will not be identical to yours, therefore do not compare your performance to yours since that's not the correct approach to use in your goal-setting. In no way. It's a distraction and one you need to get rid of right now. Your goals must be personal to you, in line with your personal priorities and desires. If other people start to become an aspect of your goal setting , that's when you've established the wrong goals for yourself.

The success of goal setting requires you to eliminate any vices you might are prone to. They are distinct from distractions. Distractions include your phone, or a social media application, perhaps even your most trusted friend who calls for a chat that could take one or two hours. These are distractions. Vices however are things you use to either to stay clear of or get rid of something. They are as harmful as excuses and you must eliminate them. In the end, finding reasons for your decisions will make it difficult to achieve your goals. As long as you continue to hold on to those vices the more difficult you're putting yourself in a position to take the actions to reach your objectives. It is important to consider what's important in terms of vices or enhancing the performance of your athletes?

The best method to track what you want to accomplish is to record your goals down. Even if it's small goals like exercising for 10 minutes more every day. No matter how small, you should write the goals down. A visual reminder to keep in mind every day reminds you of what you must be striving for. It's difficult to forget your goals when there's no way of keep track of it.

Chapter 13: Self-Discipline In School

As you've seen that people of all abilities and ages must display some degree of self-control in order to achieve their goals. This is a learned habit which, in truth, the majority of youngsters and teens learning in schools do not possess. If all students could learn to manage their behavior and track the behavior accordingly teachers would have less stress on their shoulders.

Students who exhibit the ability to maintain self-control surpass their peers overall academic performance. It has also been researched and demonstrated that students with more internal discipline exhibit wildly different behavior in a variety of ways, including being absent less frequently and performing more of the schoolwork required in addition. Students who have self-discipline were found to be more aggressive in class lessoften, and also are less likely to be a victim of alcohol and drug use.

If you want to increase your students' self-control You will have to repeatedly practice teaching methods. This chapter will present few strategies that can help your students develop to be successful and prosperous young adults.

Teaching Younger Children Self-Discipline

Self-discipline is a topic that every teacher, parent and coach is confronted with repeatedly nearly to the point of becoming the most talked about topic. What do we do as educators with regards to teaching regarding the formation for internal discipline? In order to teach our children to be successful adults, there are many factors that will require common sense in the mind. The ones who are skilled in teaching self-discipline have their own tips that have proven successful for them.

Start Early On

This principle of thumb is applicable to just about everything in the area of teaching children how to live their lives. The longer you delay on teaching children about self-control, the more bad habits will become in time. The same is true in teaching organization methods, how to play with respect, and learning to study. Even the most tiny of children can be taught to put away their toys put away.

Establish Routine

As you saw from the last chapter setting up and maintaining routines throughout the day, let children learn about self-control. Starting with washing hands to taking care of their surroundings while brushing their teeth and so on. routines are essential to developing self-discipline and making it easy to follow in daily life.

Positively Correct

If you show children how to receive criticisms and corrections without being defensive, this helps them learn faster and to not spend as much time making excuses, which allows them to get on with the next task. Self-control requires more than an ounce confidence, and therefore, as either a parent or teacher it is your responsibility to instill confidence in your children as best you can.

Encourage the Engagement in Disciplined Activities

If a child of any age is participating in activities that require an element of discipline within them and discipline, they are not only developing confidence in the process, but having fun too! Participating in plays, taking part in instruments, playing sports and so on. all contribute to developing discipline. They also give them an appreciation for their accomplishments.

Administer Success

Teachers have found that when they provide their students a step-by- stage procedure for the writing process, sketch out a picture, complete multiplication or other boring tasks, the students know how to handle the tasks more effectively. No matter if they realize that or not, kids are attracted to structure that lays out the foundation for success. Create the steps necessary to complete everyday tasks such as getting the table set, brushing teeth, cleaning their rooms and so on.

Establish Rules

Simple rules to follow can aid in the development of self-control. Set rules for you can only use your computer when homework is done, additional privileges only if the grades on their report cards are in line with your expectations, etc. If you are well and are nice in addition to being punctual, your children will respect you and are more committed to their studies.

Teach Both Short-Term and Long-Term Goals

The most difficult lessons of humanity can be the capacity to defer immediate pleasure. Instruct your children on why it's better to be happy with the outcome of a scientific project rather instead of putting off the project and watching TV instead.

Be aware that acquiring self-discipline is not an easy task.

Children are naturally impulsive miniature-humans They need what they want at the time they want it. They will try their best to convince you by using every cute smile or clever trick they employ. Be sure to let them know that you cherish you no matter what however, do not be into the trap of those puppy-dog eyes. If they slip up assist them by starting from scratch with just an bit of dismay. Human beings benefit from mistakes we make.

Strive to Be a Great Role Model

As a teacher, or parent, it is your responsibility to demonstrate to your children and students that you've mastered the importance of self-control and how you deal with it each day. In addition, you must take time to play and spend time with family members and show that when it's time to take on responsibility, you're reliable and in charge. Kids mimic our words and actions.

Teaching Methods to Reward Self-Control

If you are a teacher in students who are ruthless and disruptive students, you have to first create a space in your class that encourages self-control.

A study was conducted that gave students the option of either having one treat immediately or have two sweets later during the day. The students who chose to have two treats later in the day at later times were found to do better on tests , and less likely to take drugs. This implies that their decision to hold off on a treat depended on the way they evaluated the advantages and disadvantages in their minds.

If students have one reason not to trust the promise of a reward in the near future They tend to look for immediate satisfaction. If you can make your classroom a trusting and rewarding place and rewarding one, you'll be pleasantly surprised to observe that students are able to learn the concepts of self-discipline by themselves.

Make Self-Control a Routine

Although it might seem contradictory the most effective method for learning discipline in the classroom can be challenging the norms. There have been instances where the student's abilities to self-regulate were evaluated. That means they're required to challenge what they are taught.

The study analyzed an entire group of preschoolers who were both disciplined but not in a position to play "Red Light, Green Light." In the interest of the research the rules were changed around a bit and the children were required to play what was opposite to the game's original version, which was to put down green and move to red. What was found was that children who had already demonstrated good self-control didn't show any changes in their behavior however, those who were not as good at self-control got better. If you engage in games that go in opposition to the norms, it aids pupils who aren't as adept at self-regulation to develop self-control.

Conduct "Brain Breaks"

There are many kinds of teachers who use"brain breaks "brain break" method for many reasons. One of them is to assist students in relaxing through transitions throughout the day like recess. The breaks let students refresh and bring their concentration to tasks in between, and also help break out of the routine throughout the day.

If your child is constantly moving between tasks and on it is often difficult to maintain an uncontrolled mindset. However, when you provide them with a mental break by giving them a break, you provide them with the opportunity to recharge and refocus.

It is important to take these brain breaks during classes or other activities. They should be brief between 2 and 5 minutes total. The shorter the lessons you instruct the more they'll be able to manage themselves.

Develop Their Working Memories

"Working memory" or "working memory" for us as humans is comprised of the information is stored inside our brains. It's where you store information for a short period of time. Children who have a hard learning to master self-control are often distracted and have a difficult time to keep their focus. If you can help them improve their memory and assist them in being attentive, which helps develop self-control.

Games like Word Recall or "Memory" make the students remember the images or words they have been presented with. Another enjoyable game that students enjoy is to draw in turns. They can cover it and test if their partners can remember what they sketched.

Engaging in these kinds of games for only an hour or so each day could greatly affect the ability to work memory and self-control that your students possess.

Plan Ahead

Remember the time you had a plan in place; you most likely achieved it, didn't you? For example, if your goal was to plan a trip for the entire family, you'd list all the things you'll need for your trip. You're more likely to take your trip with ease since you're prepared for it.

The ability to plan ahead is an essential part of being disciplined. As a teacher you should ask your students to make plans for their class events or lessons, projects, or even tests. When they are more engaged in the work they do They are more likely to possess the discipline to accomplish it.

Importance of Self-Discipline in Academics

Of course, parents wish their children to perform their best and be successful in school, however it isn't a matter of just occur. It takes effort and dedication to improving your child's performance is a must, and they'll need more than just a tiny amount of self-control and discipline to achieve this. It's not just visible in the school grades, but also it is also evident in school-related behaviours that includes avoiding problematic behavior like abusing substances.

Aspects of Self-Discipline

Although self-discipline is a topic that is often discussed in schools, what is it that certain instructors and assistants don't have a good grasp of the subject?

One reason is that when this topic is discussed, a lot of people do not realize that it is connected to several personality aspects:

The signs of low impulsivity are seen in children, who are in a hurry to get their turn. They are often disruptive to others and do not sit down when it's appropriate.

The way we think, feel and actions have a major impact on the way children manage their behavior and thoughts.

The delay of reward is a further crucial element of self-control that requires a child to decline a reward that is immediate in exchange for an even bigger reward at some point in the near future.

Academics and Self-Discipline

There have been numerous research studies done by psychologists which have proved that self-discipline is the key ingredient to academic success. For instance the study was conducted on a class of middle school students where it was observed that discipline was linked with the end GPA outcomes. Tests for student achievement were more favourable as was the likelihood of being accepted into the top high schools was increased as well.

However, children who had a higher percentage of internal discipline were more disciplined at school, as well. They did not have as much time off and did more homework, spent less moments watching T.V. and began their homework early in the morning in comparison to children who had less self-discipline. Also, it was found that discipline played a role in predicting the outcome more than IQ.

Problem Behaviors and Self-Discipline

Self-control has been shown to be an integral component to academic achievement and in the classroom, it can also assist children to engage in activities that could cause an issue for school performance.

For example, a group of seventh graders was tested by psychologists as part of an experiment that tested delayed satisfaction. They asked the students whether they wanted to be paid the amount of $5 immediately or $7 at the same time next week. The students who waited for the $7 reward received higher marks than their peers who received $5 and were proven to be less likely to be involved in issues in the school environment, as well as lower rates of substance abuse.

Children with a significant delay in getting their rewards used drugs such as marijuana, cigarettes and alcohol less often than those who were looking for the $5 immediately. The study also revealed that children who were able to be patiently waiting for higher awards were more confident in themselves. This indicates that self-discipline can be linked to a variety of factors that affect the success of a school.

Self-Discipline as Children Become Teens

Self-control continues to play an essential aspect of academic achievement long after the end of the junior high school years and grade school. It is crucial for academic and professional achievement that extends beyond the teenage years. The results you learned about in this chapter are similar to those found when researchers conducted similar studies on students in the grades of nine through twelve.

In the next chapter will explore the importance of self-control and its importance for teens and young adults going to college.

Chapter 14: Preserving Your Mental Health

Even if you're mentally well, you will never be in the event that you're not doing any of the following things. You are the biggest and harshest critic. There are many different ways that you are the primary source of abuse toward your body. The people who around you can influence your thinking in the short as well as the long-term. The way you are involved in the community may help or harms your mental well-being.

Everyone would like to stay out of trouble and keep their good mental health. For those who want to improve their minds, their mental health must be the first priority before even considering lifting heavy weights. It is a good exercise your brain requires however, you must first be aware of how to care for it so that you don't risk losing the power you already possess.

No to Destructive Self-Criticism

Criticism can positive or negative. It can come from other people or you, and most of the time it comes from an inadequate self-image. How you view yourself in the present influences how you view the things around you. If you continually scold and blame yourself every time you make a mistake it's only digging deeper.

To keep from further reducing your self-esteem, you must be your most fervent admirer. But, don't be egocentric and narcissistic. Instead, you must set reasonable goals and try your best to reach these goals. Do not intentionally put yourself in a circumstance that is currently difficult to conquer or fix. If you are aware of the limits of your capabilities and what you can do to improve it, give yourself the opportunity to work within this range.

In the event that you keep trying to make and take in every negative comment the mind's development will be slowed. You'd surely like to keep expanding the scope of your mind, however, when you choose to keep a list of things you aren't able to do or the things you believe you will never accomplish, you will not achieve anything. You'll be stuck, and a great mental workout will not be possible.

Take Care of Your Body

Your mental and physical bodies are more closely linked than you imagine. If you're not getting healthy nutrition, enough rest and regular exercise due to being too lazy or simply "don't have enough time," don't expect more energy in your mind. There is no one who will be able to take better health of your body than you.

Before anyone else knows how you feel, what the source of the pain is located and the length of time you've felt it, you know that it's yours. As your body is yours is yours, you are the sole responsible for its overall health. Do not abuse your body and think it's immune to all kinds of disease and not affected by many hours of sleep deprivation. Your body isn't invincible, and your mind will not be able to develop if your body is not growing properly. It's time to live a healthier and more balanced life right now do not put off doing it.

Have Supportive Friends

The people you're in contact with directly and indirectly impact your mental wellbeing. If you're in a group of people who continually exaggerate what they aren't capable of doing or achieving the ceiling, your mind will not spread wings and take bigger leaps. If you're with people who believe in your potential and work to build your confidence your mental capabilities will expand. Additionally that your emotional stability will improve too.

A lot of unhelpful comments can be heard from a variety of places: at school, at work or even at your home. It isn't always possible to control those around your, but you can decide who becomes your closest acquaintances. You cannot control what others have to say about you However, you can alter what you hear by changing the people that tend to be around you.

Relations that aren't based on trust don't create the ideal environment for building your mind. Relationships with romantic partners can have a significant impact on how a person's brain develops. There's nothing worse than a person who doesn't believe in your abilities. Instead of displaying you to your acquaintances, you're ostracized. Do not let this unhealthy relationship last, particularly in the event that you're truly committed to developing a more positive mind. Being around someone like this each day does not help you develop your mind, it only impacts how you perceive yourself. You believe the opinions of your spouse and you lose the opportunity to develop a more productive mind.

Contribute to the Community

The community is able to benefit from every single hand willing to lend a hand. Numerous charities need the help of more people and creative minds to be more effective. However, many are reluctant to help out and allocate time to people who need help. Don't be one of those who aren't willing to take a second look. There is a chance to aid others in need and show those who are less fortunate that there is hope.

Do you realize that doing good actions or acts of kindness can boost your confidence and feelings of achievement? It's normal to people to assist each to help one another out. When you assist others, you aid yourself in seeing things in a completely different way. In some way, you could think of this new perspective as be a more precise way of seeing the world. The homeless, hungry and sick are far more numerous than the people who have satisfied their basic needs. Every day, the amount of those who are less fortunate increases. even in your own immediate vicinity you might already know people in need of help. Don't be afraid to help yourself. Your generosity will open your mind to new possibilities, and allows your mind to expand quicker.

As you allow others to profit from your sacrifices, the more liberation your mind will experience. When you make the decision to help others, you'll discover the true meaning of existence, its true meaning and the ability to change the world to the good. You want to have a more positive mind, whereas others are seeking shelter and food. This can be a win-win scenario if you are able to help others and let your new knowledge assist you.

Toughening Your Mind

This is the moment you've been looking forward to: strengthening your mental health. The previous chapters allowed you to consider the health of your mind from multiple perspectives and encouraged you to change your habits. While reading those chapters, you got a wealth of information about how to achieve more mental efficiency.

The final chapter of this guide will guide you through easy and effective ways to help strengthen your mind. Some might be more difficult than others, however the steps mentioned have been used by many and are able to help you personally experience the efficacy of exercise high-quality music, healthy diet, enough sleep, and even meditation.

Exercise, Exercise, and Exercise

You might have been informed about the importance of exercise routines to boost the brain's power. The fact is that scientific research has been conducted to establish that exercising and strengthening the mind are closely linked. The more you work out, the better the brain's performance therefore, don't be afraid to run a jog or train at the fitness center. For a stronger mind, you must strengthen your body.

While the volume of your body's muscles isn't directly affecting your brain's health, circulation can be enhanced through exercise. If you run, perform sit-ups, push-ups, or pull-ups as well as other kinds of exercises the heart beats more quickly. A rise in your heart rate is a sign of greater circulation. Fresh blood is pumped into your brain , and the oxygen-rich blood cells assist in increasing your brain's ability to process information.

Fred Gage, a researcher at The Salk Institute for Biological Studies was involved in a mouse experiment in the latter part of 1990. The mice that were exposed to wheel-running grew more intelligent. The new nerve cells that were created in their brains were formed through an increase in physical activity. The conclusion was that even those who were physically fit have better memory as the amount of neurons they possess is twice the amount of those who exercise less.

Art Kramer, a professor at the University of Illinois, also carried out an experiment to prove that exercising improves brain performance. He conducted his research on a study showing that the hippocampus, a part of the brain responsible for memory and learning shrinks by one-to-two percent each year for those who don't suffer from dementia. It means that even people who don't have any neurological issues lose their efficiency as age gets older.

Kramer invited a few people to join a year-long walk program for a year. In the beginning of the trial, they went through an MRI to assess how big their hippocampus. After a year, the participants who had completed the walk were examined another time with Kramer. Kramer found that the hippocampi of the people who completed the task grew by 2 percent. They also had better memory despite their rather old age.

It's clear that walking is a great way to stimulate your brain. Avoid getting too cozy in a cab or public transport. Instead, do a few extra steps each day and work out regularly to boost the brain's effectiveness. If you're seeking a more powerful body, allow your mind to move more often and move away from your couch and several bags filled with potato chips.

Listen to Classical Music

Music is powerful, perhaps far more powerful than people think. That's why it's crucial to be careful about the music you play. There are many kinds of music in the world however the most beneficial one for improving mental well-being can be described as "classical."

It is true that classical music can improve your brain's efficiency. Many psychologists refer to it as"the "Mozart Effect," in the sense that people from all age group can benefit from having their thinking abilities and thinking patterns enhanced by listening to Mozart's two piano concertos. Beethoven, Tchaikovsky, Bach and a host of other artists and composers that hail from in the Baroque and Classical times have also created pieces that help with the development of the brain.

If you'd like to experience greater ease processing things by your brain, allow Classical music play in your ears to help your brain function. The complicated and "rigorous" order of the music of the famous Classical composers helps increase the production of serotonin within the brain. Serotonin is a substance that aids your brain in thinking more efficiently, which allows you to process information faster.

Eat Healthy

Food choices affect your thoughts patterns. If you continue to eat junk food, which actually contains much more harmful substances in comparison to the nutrients your body requires, your mind is bound to weak points. In the book, healthy nutrition can helps you think.

Minerals and vitamins have different effects on the mental well-being of your family, however they all contribute to enhance your overall health. A variety of foods are thought to be beneficial for the brain. Fish that are rich in iron poultry that is rich in protein as well as fruits and vegetables that are high in fiber as well as a variety of minerals and vitamins can dramatically improve the efficiency of your brain.

Get Adequate Sleep

People who are less sleepy, are more susceptible to losing weight than they realize. The body uses sleep to replenish strength and to heal wounds. If you're not sleeping then your brain won't have time to organize your thoughts or process relevant details more deeply. In one of the earlier chapters, dreams were associated with self-discovery. What can you do to dream even if you're not getting enough rest? Recover and experience the advantages of letting your brain get stronger while you sleep.

Meditation

Meditation can help you see numerous things that are unnoticed when you're busy with a variety of work issues as well as school and family concerns. When you tackle every issue with a straight face, without even taking a moment to think about them You won't be as effective as you could be. If you can calm your mind and allow it to rest, it gives it the chance to tell you what should be prioritised. Many renowned yoga teachers say, "There's value in silence." Be quiet each now and then to help strengthen it considerably.

Chapter 15: Time Management

This is a continuation of previous chapters. I've already explained to you to be aware of what you are doing and how to eliminate distractions. I've also advised that you should turn off any the media that could cause you to be disturbed. This chapter I'd like to push you to the limit and it's a huge task. From from your mind, I'd like you to describe the length of time you've spent in every week doing the following:
• Catching up on social media
* Watching the TV
• Sitting inside your vehicle while you wait
* Stressing about events that haven't actually happened as of yet
How do you determine that with respect to time? From today you'll have an notebook along and record the time of your day you are occupied with things that are not productive. The time you spend on these activities is wasted. If you've got an

enduring favorite show on TV, there's absolutely no reason to not go to the theater but you should turn off the TV afterward. What are you feeling about social media? Is it important how often you check in on your notifications? It's true, but it's useless and wastes time. Turn off your notifications. If you'd like to dedicate an hour or so in the evening , to Facebook and the other associated accounts, you should set the time aside for a specific period of time and go through the accounts.

What can you do to fulfill the promise you have promised yourself that you will do when you're stuck in traffic? What about enjoying and listening to music? What is it like to learn another language? How can this make you more mentally tough? People who have a good time management strategy appear to be able to achieve much better than average Joe. They are aware that they're given a certain amount of time per day, and they make sure to not waste their time. Take a look at the waste of time. I remember the first time I made this mistake I was shocked and I was spending three hours per day doing things with no purpose whatsoever. When you multiply that over the course of one year, that's the majority of your time which is spent. Make time for it to allow you to stick on track with your goals in time management.

Utilizing Time Management to reach your objectives

If you're aware of the time you are wasting in your day You are then capable of replacing waste with efficiency. So, when you need to complete something you will have the time needed to complete it. Have you been amazed by people who are able to help you in a flash without showing any signs of dislike? There is a good chance that you have been awed by these people, and they have a strong mental stamina and are are able to respond to events when they arise. If you set targets for yourself and strive to complete them by their deadline What you're doing is showing yourself that you are capable of. It's not a way to impress other people. It's simply about adjusting your schedule to accommodate more work. Let's take a examine how this is accomplished.

Create a list of five goals you'll need to accomplish in the next day. Next, take note of the behaviors that are on your list of waste of time. They will be the things you will only be able to do once you have completed your obligations. Thus, the quicker you can get your obligations out of the way then the more likely you will be to be able to take pleasure in your hobbies. The list should be made at the beginning of the day. Consider what you have to complete until midday. If you are faced with the deadline at 11:11 change it to a deadline of 10 o'clock. What you should do when you do this is to alter your attitude and force yourself to do something prior to time. They are basically deadlines you make yourself, so that when the real deadlines come into the picture, you'll have the proper mindset to meet these deadlines before the date you have set. The benefit of this is that in the event that adjustments have needed, you're not in a rush and can easily make them.

They know how to effectively use their time. My time management system is comprised of the following:

Things I am required to complete within a certain date.

Things I'd like to do

Extra things that I can help make easier

Time for me

So, I'm making allowances every day for additional tasks, even if they're not expected from me. However, I make sure there's some time set aside for me. I require that time to remain mentally strong. Without this time I am able to give myself little. If I can complete other work in time, I can increase the amount of time I spend with myself and not feel guilty about it.

Your time should also be devoted to obligations to others, activities that you are involved in, phone calls you have to make, and letters that you have to get caught up on. If you're not able to keep track of your time and accomplish every task scheduled to you, it is easy to lose interest in timekeeping and begin to put off tasks. Then, trouble begins to set in.

Utilize the goal-setting method I mentioned earlier to determine what you have to accomplish in your daily life. It is possible to add your fun activities whenever you have free moment, however you have to do a specific amount every day to earn income to live a better life. It is now time to eliminate the waste of time, and find out how much more you can accomplish when you turn off all the distracting things. You'll be surprised.

The issues people face with timekeeping can be multi-faceted. If you fail at the goal you want, you'll be hesitant to attempt it over again. You must change your mental attitude and recognize that there are times it takes longer than you thought to complete the task. If everyone within the hierarchy of command understands the reason behind the delay, it's not a problem in the overall plan of the things. Prioritizing tasks helps you select the most important tasks to accomplish within a certain time. It is also a good idea to consider that setting aside time for tasks that are difficult is a great idea, and it should be done at the beginning of the day or right after returning from lunch as these are the time when your mind is not stressed and has enough energy to focus on challenging tasks. It is important to ensure that you are sleeping regularly and do not miss this part of your life. This is as during the healing process the mind is stimulated for the coming day. And If you don't get enough sleep and you don't get enough sleep, you're likely to be sluggish when you wake up.

If you are able to have your time properly managed, it excites you. You are happy with your accomplishments and are prepared to tackle your next accomplishments. The people who are mentally strong know what happens when they don't it's the world telling them there has to be a different way of doing things. It's a lesson instead of something negative. Therefore, shifting your perspective to a positive attitude in tackling your schedule and schedule for your day are crucial. If you change your approach, you'll learn much about the task that was a bit daunting the previous day.

Chapter 16: Developing Your Discipline With These Simple Methods

Discipline can be the key to success or failure. If you're not disciplined and discipline, it is less likely that you will be successful because of your lack of motivational skills. If you don't have self-motivation, you'll realize that your dreams and goals are not achievable.

When you are able to improve your skills to improve your mental strength as well as your discipline. If you can do this then, you could achieve your goals more quickly.

Remove All Temptations

There are temptations everywhere. They are in the form of food, television shows and much more. But, it's these temptations that will hinder you from achieving the discipline you desire and require.

You have to be mentally strong , but when you're not able to resist temptations and develop a the art of the art of discipline, it will be difficult to be able to achieve it. If you keep temptations at your fingertips this tests your discipline, but most of the time you'll be able to win. Instead, get rid of them.

Set Small Goals

Every person has a goal and , even if it seems to be far off, it is possible for it to be attainable. All you need to do is create small goals. If you establish smaller goals, you will begin to work towards them slowly, but steadily.

Let's say that you'd like to be an actor. The first step would be setting the goal of going to the drama class. When you've achieved the desired goal, you would set another. By taking small steps, you are able to remain focused and disciplined to the task that is at hand.

The bigger goals are often the cause of your to wander off the path. To keep your discipline You must establish smaller objectives.

Take Your Time

The process of becoming mentally tough takes time, as does establishing your self-control levels. If you hurry to get things done, you'll hit the roadblock that puts back time by months. They may be harmful, however there is no need to hurry.

It is possible to slowly but steadily build up your mental strength and increase your discipline. There will be setbacks, but as you begin to build self-control and discipline, you must take things slowly to avoid making mistakes.

The more you push yourself and push yourself, the more powerful you will become.

Focus Positively On Goals

Goals can be formulated and you must be able to think about them positively. By focusing on your goals, you will help you develop discipline towards those things that you must avoid. Staying positive and focusing on positive actions will help you to establish discipline.

Find What Makes You Motivated the Most

To stay disciplined, you must learn more about your own self. You ought to be aware of what drives you, but if not now, you must start! You need to learn about your desires, your urges and what motivates you to take action and get out of bed.

If you have certain things that you know you won't be able to resist, then you need to beware of them.

Have Willpower

To become more mentally strong You must build your determination. This will also help in the development of discipline. Willpower is a key ingredient to reaching goals, and will help you build your mental strength too.

Set a Good Routine

Breaking up a routine can be beneficial in many ways , but it's also possible to develop one. If you decide to set the routine, you'll add your favorite things to do the most, as well as those things that keep you motivated. This will allow you to achieve your objectives.

Say No!

There will be feelings, thoughts and desires, but it's those things that can will lead you to the wrong track. Instead, you need to learn to say no in a more thoughtful manner and learn to recognize the right thing to do and what's not. It may be difficult to say"no" at first, but it'll be worthwhile.

If you're looking to shed weight, avoid desserts for two days every week. If you're looking to build your muscles by exercising, do so for an extra day. There are a myriad of actions you can take to increase your mental endurance and boost your discipline as well.

Picture Your Rewards

Nothing is more effective to improve your discipline than to imagine your goals. I guarantee you that pictures are powerful tools and is important to think about your goals.

Determination Is a Powerful Tool to Build Your Mental Toughness

The process of becoming mentally stronger is always going to be a challenge. There will be times you think you are able to conquer the world, and other times, you're engulfed in the flames. It's not easy, however, to be the person you'd like to become, you have to develop resilience and determination.

Fear can be a drag and prevents you from achieving however, it is all comes down to mental toughness. It is essential to have a strong mental state since when you are in an enviable mental state that is determined, this will help you stay on the right path towards success.

How do you increase your determination through resiliency?

Stop Believing Crises Are Unsolvable Problems

There will be times when stressful events happen. they can't be changed, but you can modify the way you respond to these situations. Anybody can change how they react to crisis situations, including you, and it's simple to change your approach.

Instead of viewing an awful situation from a negative perspective Instead, you concentrate on the positive. Do not get trapped in a rut and think there's no way out of this crisis otherwise , you'll be stuck. It is important to be optimistic about the end result and look forward towards the future as well.

Negatives can be turned into a positive in the most dire of circumstances. It is your responsibility to ensure that you are able to find the positives. Simple modifications could make all the difference and you should stop thinking that there's no way out of a negative situation.

Stay Resilient With Acceptance

Acceptance is an essential part of life . While you may not agree with the situation however, you need to be able how to deal with it. When you are able to accept a difficult circumstance, you are able to get over it. There is a chance to resolve the issue and proceed with your life.

If you're looking to cry, do it, but when you've stopped you must stand up and tell yourself that you're moving forward.

Take Action

The ability to be decisive is an attribute for all people and you should be able to demonstrate this. If you're adamant you are able to get up and act. It is not a good idea to just sit back and hope in anticipation of something happening, because when you do that you wait, it won't happen. Instead, you should be proactive now and making sure you take positive steps.

Look For Opportunities

Opportunities may not always appear before you, so whenever they come up, take advantage of them and never let go!

Even the smallest of opportunities can open doors to you. It is important to be able to recognize any opportunity that is presented and also create opportunities.

Planning

There will be bad things that happen and you'll be faced with difficult situations every day. But, if you're looking to improve your resilience it is important to plan for the worst scenarios so that you can recover. It's not difficult to accomplish.

Know Where You Want To Go and Be Specific

Every leader knows the goals they'd like to achieve and you should follow the same path. It is important to be aware of where you're heading in order to be able to reach your goals. If you don't, you'll never get anywhere.

Additionally, you must be specific in your goals. Do not be vague; try to be specific as it will help you remain focused and precise. This is crucial to create a strong strategy and strengthen your determination as well.

Set Out a Time and Reward Your Goals

The deadline isn't always the most effective solution for you but in order to keep you focused it is essential to adhere according to deadlines. This will help you be a lot more productive, maintain your concentration and build your emotional strength.

To remain focused You must remain positive and give rewards. If you accomplish something great you can you should reward yourself. It helps keep the motivation up.

Chapter 17: Being Controlled By Others

This is the shadow side of the outside world. Like we each have our own personal shadow , the entire world operates with a balance between dark and light. Control is a clear sign of a dysfunctional mental and physical relationship. The results can be catastrophic in your pursuit of fitness and mental endurance.

Why do others seek control? To answer this question of the soul first, we must consider the question of power. What are you thinking of as you consider power? Political leaders, bosses, fame, money, status? Do you think of mental or physical competence, like an ace chess player could possess or an army captain? Do you imagine tools or machines that possess strong strength and the capability to kill? Do you picture your parent? Perhaps a close friend?

The most amazing spiritual fact is that all human beings are able to access unending power. This isn't the way the world would like you to think. The world divides power to ensure that certain people enjoy plenty of it and others are not worthy. The power that the 'deserving' are able to wield is both incredibly and real. The dictators can take families down by a single command. Wall Street titans can bend the economic system to suit their needs and parents who are both compassionate and harsh can influence the way they treat their children's lives. The problem is that these aren't manifestations of power. they are all displays of control.

Control is a false attempt to take over another's control.

The real power lies within, and it's light and love. Consider an instance of kindness. Perhaps it was a time when you gave someone your time and attention, or where someone showed kindness towards you. The intensity of the relationship between the two people is felt as more than the moment. A feeling of empathy and connection that you feel when handing someone in the street a dime or the warmth you feel when someone offers help when you fall down and fall: that is the real power. True power is that energy that binds all beings with a sense of affection. The notion that a person of another nation is different from one you are could be empowering idea. The work and literature on empowerment is about reminding that you're made of beautiful, tough material and that there is more to your existence than the present circumstances. It is a kind of energy that does not ask for anything from anyone because this knowledge of the universe is linked to everything simultaneously. Everyone has the capacity to tap into this unending amount of love and connections anytime regardless of.

The issue begins by acknowledging that being human, and this spiritual truth within is hard. Self-esteem, vanity, and insecurities are a given. There are physical aspects of existence that cannot be ignored. The power of money is a key component to attain status and wealth and is accessible by a lack of understanding. The issue lies in the fact that society doesn't financially reward connections to actual power, yet that ever give you the illusion of perception of it.

People, due to being evolutionaryally adaptive, can make others up. Are you large enough to be able to beat me up and steal my dinner? If so, I'll be watching out for you. Are you snooping around and seeking to steal my friend? I'll ensure that your life is in a state of chaos first. All of this leads to the power-plays that follow and power-assessments. The first step is to look around the world to find out who's got what you want and what you are looking for, or what you think you require or would like. Then, you determine how you can remove the power of another person or advantage, in order to achieve your goals. I'll cause you to live a nightmare at work since you've made me seem an employee difficult and I'm not going to let me lose my self-esteem. You'll say you're raising your daughter with a lack of discipline because you're incapable of believing she is more in love with me than. Do you see how messy, dirty and dark these are?

They all contribute to attempting to control others to gain "power". They're all just exhausting plans to seize the appearance of power in order to compensate the perceived deficiency. Imagine any of these scenarios viewed with the knowledge that there is unlimited inner power that is a result of love. Now, tell me you believe that I'm raising our daughter in a way that is lacking discipline because you are seeing that she's hurting for more discipline and boundaries and you are in love with me, and you want only the best for us both. us. A much more productive discussion can be initiated. An issue at work is dealt with directly and without any passive aggressiveness. All feelings are discussed and removed.

Control is a sly tactic since it's never beneficial to anyone. It is possible to believe that you are getting a benefit from having control over the outcome to your advantage however it is draining valuable resources since you're ignoring your inner beliefs. It is possible to be nice to someone to secure an improved table in for dinner but a small part of you is aware that you gave away part of your character to win a pointless prize.

Weed Out the Power-Players

Don't let yourself be controlled by others. Unfortunately, there are many who don't recognize that they are being controlled by the society. It is commonplace for people to seek to please other people rather than yourself. However, there are different ways in which you could become a victim of others. However, you need to be aware that if you let the situation to occur, you won't be in a position to live your life. Instead, it's those around you that are going to lead your life. This is a recipe for to feel stressed and exhausted. This may take on a variety of ways, like the fact that others stop you from following your goals or the desire to please others or influence from your family, social circle, peers and friends media, and many more. Whatever the reason or the way you are influenced by others it is important to recognize that it is essential to determine your own self-worth and identify. Learn to say no to people who attempt to alter your life. There is a good chance that many of them will attempt to alter you believing that it's the right option. Be aware that no matter what you hear from someone else or anything they say, think of every suggestion as a suggestion. It's your choice if you'll allow yourself to be guided by the views of other people. Again, it is your responsibility to have complete control over your life.

One common mistake is to rely on the advice of others in order to place blame on them when the results don't work positively. This is not a good thing since it is impossible to take blame on others. You must be able to take your own choices and take responsibility for all consequences for your actions. Placing the blame on others won't change your circumstances, so begin accepting responsibility for your choices and actions.

A few people are satisfied from pleasing other people by letting them control their lives. This is, however, an illusion of happiness. In time, you'll be feeling a sort of emptiness that is present in your heart, some sort of unsatisfied desire. If this happens, it is an indication that you've been unable to live your life as you wanted it to be. Naturally, this may leave you feeling disappointed and exhausted. Don't allow other people to live their lives for you. Do not rely on anyone else to tell you what you should do.

It's Never Too Late to Say No

But, what happens if your life is being controlled by other people? What do you do? In this instance you need to make positive changes and take a stand for yourself. It is time to not be a slave to people who attempt to influence you, and start living the life you've always dreamed of. This may not be simple to do, particularly when people who surround you are accustomed to instructing you on what you should do. However, it's vital that you stand up for yourself. If you don't remove yourself from the pressures of others, you'll always be exhausted. This is because you'll never be content because you're doing nothing, but accepting the dictates of others on what you do in it. It is not necessary to have to be in an argument to achieve this. It is important to know how to stand up and defend your position without fighting or being a thorn in the side. Be calm and respectful. Keep in mind that you don't have to explain yourself to anyone. There are some people who may not get it and may think negatively about you and not bother. A lot of times they are those who aren't fully in charge of their lives and spend their lives trying to please others. Don't be like them. To control your life, you just must be certain of your own self. You don't need the approval or consent of other people. This is the way to effectively control your life. There are some people who do what others say to them. This is often done so they will find someone else to blame should their plan not come through at the final. But this is not the right way to go and can be a tragedy. It is impossible to escape responsibility by trying to blame another person. At the end of the day, you're solely accountable for your own life and all that takes place in it. Thus, take charge and control your life. To control your destiny, you must to control your life. Do not blame others and accept on the entire responsibility.

At first you may feel very uncomfortable, especially if you are used to listening to what others tell you. Butdon't be worried as you'll soon be familiar with the process.

Before you can take charge over your own life you must first establish a course for yourself. Being in control implies positive actions. So, it is essential to be aware of yourself and what you wish to occur within your own life. In this way, you'll be aware of your direction and direction. However, if you do not know who you are and you're not even sure of the goals you'd like to accomplish and why, you might not feel like you're in control of anything. This is due to a lack of direction. If you become accustomed to relying on others for validation or an idea of what you should do and you set yourself up to be disappointed. You must be adamant and establish the direction for your life. This is the moment to get everything in order. Do not look at others for proof, and choose your own way. There's no need to rush. You are free to take the time you'll need to come up with a choice you'll be happy with and adhere to.

Processing the Grief of Letting Controlling People Go

The most common problem is not realizing that you are being controlled by others. It is important to recognize. Therefore, look at your life at the moment. Are there aspects of your life you would like to alter? Be honest and open to yourself. What areas that you live with are out that are your responsibility? Make sure to be as precise as you can. Find the people who seem to have a direct influence on your life. Do they serve as a sources of inspiration or do they cause you to struggle? Spend as much time as you can to comprehend your life situation and be aware of your personal circle or people closest to you. Consider that there's a difference between being accountable or being controlled by others. If, for instance, there is a family it is your duty to provide for your family. It is not a good idea to free yourself from others to escape your obligations.

Do you have to hate those who are trying to take over your life? It's not a good idea. The majority of them are looking for what they believe is most beneficial for you. Actually, the majority times the reason they attempt to influence or guide your actions in life is that they are concerned about the people around them. So, they provide you with "suggestions." Although there instances when they appear as a command to obey but it's your decision whether or not you'll listen to them or not. Furthermore, they cannot influence you without your approval. You remain fully in your training and exercising your personal freedom It's just that you have to make it work better.

When you finally make the decision to try to take control over your life, rather than having others guide your course, you're likely to be faced with some obstacles. Don't get discouraged when you face challenges along the way however, be confident that you'll succeed when you do your best. It could take some time to adapt. Be sure to discover your real feeling of self-confidence and power. If you complete this step you will be returning to the core conviction that your power is based on only you. Your power is, at its center, the power of the love and connection. The actions you take that show and believe in this belief will give you a greater sense of your own self and a feeling of being free from the pressures of others.

Chapter 18: Tips And Tricks

In the final part in this article, we'll discuss certain behaviors and strategies that you can apply right away to ensure you have the best running experience.

A Runner's Meal

Insufficient nutrition can affect your performance, impede your progress, and will not benefit your health in any way. The food you should consume is different in relation to what you're doing.

Casual Runs - If you run at an average speed of less than one hour, you'll probably be fine without much more than drinking a glass of water to make sure you're well hydrated. If you're feeling hungry, you can try the banana or Granola bar. It is recommended to consume the food between 2 and 3 hours prior to a workout (People digest differently which is why you should adjust this if it's not for your needs). Once you're done, consume something within the next couple of hours, in order to keep from feeling fatigued or sick. Anything that contains protein or fiber would be ideal. Protein shakes are excellent if you're in a hurry.

Rapid runs - If your working to the limit and speedily, you'll burn through energy like a monster. It is essential to eat before and after. A few carbs that are digestible, like toast along with jelly fruit smoothie is a good idea. It is recommended to consume 200-400 calories dependent on many factors such as gender, age and height -ideal is 45 minutes to one hour prior to the workout. After you've finished it's essential to eat food for 30 minutes in order to replenish the body. Choose fluids carbohydrates, protein and carbs.

Long-distance runs require the greatest planning because you'll have to eat throughout, before and after. You won't be able to successfully complete a 10K run for instance without having a variety of energy boosts during the course. This is where energy gels, block beans, chews and other chews are essential. The general rule is that every hour that is over 75 minutes, you should consume between 30 and 60 grams of carbohydrates. They must be consumed in liquid, otherwise they'll be sat in your stomach like a rock and travel into your body in a slow manner. Some take it all in one go, but having your fuel in small pieces, like each 15 minute interval, can keep your levels stable and help avoid digestive problems.

You should eat no more than one hour prior to when you begin. If you eat earlier, you risk exhausting your energy and is very difficult recovering from. After your run, a drink or drink that contains four parts carbs to one portion protein is ideal to help you get back in the right direction. Like the fast run it should take no more than 30 minutes or 45 minutes maximum. After your stomach has settled down, opt for some carbs that are heavy such as oatmeal, basmati rice, as well as whole-grain pasta.

Proper Hydration

If you didn't notice during your workout you sweat. When this happens, the volume of blood decreases which means that your heart must be working more to pump blood and give your muscles the oxygen they require.

The biologist's view. This is the running version In the event that you don't drink enough fluids, you'll become dehydrated and uncomfortable while running.

It's true that most people do not drink enough water. The ideal intake of water is approximately half of your body's weight in ounces every day. (ex: 150lbs = 75 oz.) When do you drink and what drink should you have?

The majority of the time, water is fine. The sports drinks supply minerals, sodium and some extra energy, which can be helpful for long or intense runs. If you're running faster or higher than usual, it's the perfect time to drink the Gatorade or other drinks you like. If you're running for 30 minutes or less it is possible to manage without any drinks in any way unless it's extremely hot outside. If you drink well during the course of the day, dehydration will not be a problem until an hour into a typical run.

Do not try filling up your tank with the same speed as an automobile prior to a run. In the event that you try, the entire liquid will make you feel sluggish when you begin running. It is heavy and it can make you feel heavier in the event that you exceed your limit. Many runners prefer to have the option of having a "pit stop" on their route, for example, an convenience store, or their own home. For long distance runs it's a must. Bring a bottle along If you'd like and switch your grip if you feel it is slipping after some time. Utilizing a belt with fluids can be a great alternative.

Easy & Cheap Foot Massage

If you have the money massage therapists can do wonders for your feet. For those who don't an lacrosse ball may give you some relief at home on your feet. The golf ball can also be used well. A tennis ball can be used however it offers more power than a lacrosse ball making it more suitable for deep tissue massage.

It's really not that complicated. Simply place the ball underneath an arch in your foot and then roll your feet over it. This should be done until you reach a level of ease. The ball should offer immediate relief, especially if you have arch muscles that are tight. One tip is keeping a ball from lacrosse on frozen ice so that the cold will help to reduce swelling after running. It is possible that you will enjoy this foot massage that is cold enough to apply it following every run. Some runners prefer the full capacity of a water bottle from the refrigerator. It's awkward in comparison, however many runners appreciate the plastic's elasticity and the coldness. It's all about the preference.

Sometimes, running is an actual pain on the back. If your glutes are aching it is possible that the lacrosse ball will aid in this area as well. When you stand, place the ball between your cheeks and a wall, placing the ball placed on top of the area that is painful. Put your butt in the wall, then move the ball in a circular movement around the affected area. Make it appear as if your butt's a rag and the wall is like a window you're cleaning. If the pain is lessening you can stop the movement and put the ball in on the floor between your wall and the painful area. Put your foot into the ball and keep it for 30 minutes.

When to Replace Your Running Shoes

Running shoes last an average of 300-500 miles depending on how vigorous you're using them. The more effectively your foot is the better, the greater wear you'll get from your running shoes. Take note of how your feet feel. If you've worn the shoes for more than 300 miles and they feel that they're not offering adequate protection, you're most likely correct. If you're not sure you should give it some time. On one day, you could feel tired. Three days of fatigue is a pattern that requires to be addressed. If you notice middlesole materials of white peeking out or the sole appears to be cracked it's likely that you've waited for too long and are in need of the replacement of your pair.

Chapter 19: Where There's A Will

There's A Way

When we are thinking of willpower, many usually imagine dieting.

We are thinking of that wonderful chunk of chocolate cake we have in the refrigerator, and how wonderful that it is to get one piece. We imagine what we'd like to see at ourselves in the mirror and what we'd like to see when looking at the size.

However, there's much greater to having willpower that simply saying "no" to something you enjoy. There are many occasions when your the test of your willpower will be an assessment of your ability generally and you'll be content to give up what you're fighting to get a slice of cake.

Whatever service you select it is likely that you will have to endure weeks of long hours, no sleep, a lack of food, and the absence of any amenities you've grown used to.

Even if you choose to enter an area that is quite common, for instance, medical where you'll be required to work for long hours and very little rest, and perform surgeries and other life-saving procedures if you're not eating anything to eat. You will be required to demonstrate optimism and enthusiasm even when you're exhausted and then decide when to go home to and sleep.

One of the best indicators of mental strength is the capacity to put the needs of others before your own and to think about the things you can accomplish to make them happy prior to worrying about what will bring you joy.

There are occasions where your comfort is paramount but not when you're trapped in a foreign location or working to find a solution to a problem or you're battling time for a surgery that is much more delicate that you imagined you'll know the meaning of putting other people above you.

If you fight the urge to sleep, eat or get cool, warm off, change your clothes or whatever else you're habitually doing you'll be being tested. Your body is likely be a rebel However, you need to keep your vigilance.

Like the other aspects I've been highlighting it, too, is something that requires the time required and efforts. At this moment, you might believe that you are unable to sacrifice something you're looking forward to. Perhaps you're on the other side of the spectrum and are expecting that it will be much simpler than it actually is.

Whatever it is you want to experience You will need to go through it personally before you get a sense of what it really is like. Chances are that you'll need to practice and improve your skills before you are able to declare yourself to be a master in this particular field.

Keep in mind that the more you are working on it and the more often you're forced to abandon the routine comforts you've been accustomed to, the more comfortable it will be to be over time. It may not seem like much enjoyment in the moment but if you persevere to it, it's likely to be so simple that you don't even know you're working out your willpower until someone mentions it to you.

Then things become simpler.

Chapter 20: The Most Powerful Skill You Can Learn: Setting Goals

The ability to set goals correctly is perhaps the most valuable skill you can master. Why? because it allows you to accomplish an array of other objectives. If you are able to define goals, it will allow you to work towards any goal. This is the most important factor to unlocking almost everything you'd like from your life.

The first thing you need to concentrate on is setting goals! But until now, you've likely been doing everything in the wrong way...

The Problem With Your Current Goals

What can be the reason a goal could be incorrect?

Yes, any goal is worth pursuing But the way you define your goals and organize them will dramatically increase your odds of success.

Let's consider the weight loss illustration since it's among the most straightforward goals that is easy to accomplish.

If you are looking to shed some weight, it is important to start with a clear target. The typical goal will look like this:

"Lose 2 stone by next year" This is an awful target. Why? The first reason is that it's too unclear. What are you doing to lose weight? What is your source of weight loss? What are the reasons you'd like to shed some weight? What do you wish to look like?

However you're not in control. Even if you're fully determined to achieve your goals You may discover external forces hinder your success. You might get sick or you follow the wrong path, or perhaps you discover that you're not eating enough!

The final target is far off away. If you're trying to lose weight by the end of the year, then that lets you put off doing it. The goal is so far off, that you can indulge in a bit of overeating or postpone exercising for a time and don't think about it until the next month.

Six months go by and you realise that you're still far than you thought. Because it's now too late, you'll probably simply give up now.

This is not a very good objective!

* What Good Goals Look Like

So, what would an effective objective be like? How can you frame the same goal in a way that will improve your odds of getting it done?

The first step is to concentrate on the things you can immediately control and not influenced by external influences whatsoever. The goals you set should be ones that you can achieve with certainty and will be assessed immediately in a pass-fail manner.

For instance instead of trying to lose 2 stone next year, set this objective: "I will work out three times a week, every week, for at least 15 minutes"

This is an objective to strive for. No matter what your metabolism is or the risk of injury or any other external factor that may hinder you, this is an objective you are able to achieve. Also, you shouldn't put off the goal . It also ensures that you never reach the embarrassing point where you never have a chance of reaching the task. At any time during your journey, there's no reason why you shouldn't begin to work towards this goal and hope to succeed.

By focusing on this tiny, short-term objective, you'll realize that the longer-term goal of losing weight will take into consideration.

* How to Formulate Your Goals

But that doesn't mean any goal in the short term that's non-binary will be able to meet it.

In the first place, you must know what you are looking for and ensure that the objective you set for yourself will assist you in reaching it. It is essential for your goals to be motivating to the core, and that implies that you need to be genuinely enthusiastic about them. If you've only pursued an objective that you are excited about that you'll discover you've got the motivation and drive to continue.

Doing 15 minutes of exercise every day is a great target because it's guaranteed to help you get closer to your larger objective in losing fat. If you keep that objective in mind, you'll be more likely to being motivated to exercise even when you're tired or weak and sluggish.

You shouldn't aim to lose weight', either. Instead, you need to have a better understanding of what this means. Do you want to become slimmer? Do you wish to be more athletic? What is the reason you're interested in that thing? Are you hoping that you'll be more attractive to someone else's sexual partner? Perhaps you're looking for more energy? Take a look at yourself honestly and pay attention to the drive in your body which is driving you towards your goal. attain.

If your aim is to earn money, concentrate on the motivational factor that drives you to want to earn that money. It's likely to boil down to more than money - perhaps you're looking for status? Power? Confidence? Freedom? Only when you truly understand the nature of your goals will you be able to a) follow the fastest path to achieve them, and b) retain the determination and enthusiasm that you'll require to achieve your goals.

This will require some soul-searching!

Furthermore, you should make sure that your goals you have set are achievable and realistic and that you've divided them up into smaller enough steps. Example: Our goals for losing weight are to exercise for 15 minutes every day. This is a small amount, but it's realistic and achievable. If you attempt to make your goals more difficult - like doing an hour of exercise per day - you'll find yourself immediately disappointed when you are unable to make the time or desire to do it. It's easy to put off exercise and find excuses. The greatest thing about working out in just 15 minutes of time is the fact that once you get started it's not uncommon to take longer.

Think about it this way It's more beneficial to set a smaller easily-to-achieve goal and then stick to it than to set a huge life-changing goal you aren't able to manage!

Of course when you make your goals smaller, it implies that it's going to take longer to reach the final destination you're aiming for. This isn't an issue: it's one more thing that you have to accept if you wish to do any thing. Things that matter take time. Make small steps that are steady and take your time enjoying the journey.

Conclusion

Making new habits can be difficult. Take small steps at a. The time required to develop new habits can vary based on the difficulty and the commitment to make it happen. It is your responsibility to choose one thing to do and then take action. Simply taking action is a step to improve oneself. You can do it!

www.ingramcontent.com/pod-product-compliance
Lightning Source LLC
Chambersburg PA
CBHW071841080526
44589CB00012B/1079